I Seek Truth

TALKING *to Your* HEAVENLY FATHER
ABOUT FINDING TRUTH IN LIFE

TERRY SQUIRES

WORTHY®
PUBLISHING

New York • Nashville

Worthy
Hachette Book Group
1290 Avenue of the Americas, New York, NY 10104

worthypublishing.com
twitter.com/worthypub

First Edition: February 2019

Worthy is a division of Hachette Book Group, Inc. The Worthy name and logo are trademarks of Hachette Book Group, Inc.

The publisher is not responsible for websites (or their content) that are not owned by the publisher.

Published in association with Ted Squires.

Unless otherwise noted, Scripture quotations are taken from The Holy Bible, English Standard Version® (ESV®) Copyright © 2001 by Crossway, a publishing ministry of Good News Publishers. | Scripture quotations marked NASB are taken from New American Standard Bible® Copyright © 1960, 1962, 1963, 1968, 1971, 1972, 1973, 1975, 1977, 1995 by The Lockman Foundation. | Scripture quotations marked NIV are taken from The Holy Bible, New International Version®, NIV® Copyright © 1973, 1978, 1984, 2011 by Biblica, Inc. | NIV One Impact Bible Notes used by permission of Terry Squires, copyright © 2012 Terry Squires.

Cover design by Chris Gilbert, Gilbert & Carlson Design. Art Credit: shutterstock.com.| Robyn Mackenzie. Print book interior design by Bart Dawson.

Library of Congress Control Number: 2018964436

ISBN: 978-1-68397-298-3 (hardcover)

Printed in the United States of America

LAKE

10 9 8 7 6 5 4 3 2 1

To my husband, Ted—
a man who impacts the world
by standing firm on God's truth.

Acknowledgments

I'd like to express my heartfelt gratitude to those who brought *I Seek Truth* to life:

Kay Arthur—You are my gift from God.

Jeana Ledbetter—A special thank you for embracing *I Seek Truth*.

Byron Williamson, Jeana Ledbetter, Marilyn Jansen, and all the staff at Worthy Publishing.

And to all my dear friends who are speaking truth into the lives of others.

Contents

Introduction

Ever since Adam's fall in the garden, every one of us has experienced trials resulting from our sins that separate us from our heavenly Father. We search for meaning but can't find it. We work to be good but fail. We look for hope but find ourselves lost.

My friend, are you searching for truth in your life but your tears are blinding you from seeing Jesus, who is standing right in front of you? Has the world pulled you away from God by enticing you to believe that others have the answers that will bring you happiness? Our Father is calling you to seek His face, His Word—the Bible—and His promises that will fulfill your life—His truth.

I Seek Truth is an intimate journey of ninety devotions that are heartfelt conversations with our heavenly Father. Each devotion is written in first person so that you can identify with each topic. From Genesis to Revelation, *I Seek Truth* will encourage you to seek and know God's Word and His truth for your life.

My prayer is that His Word will speak to your heart and that you will know He has done great things through the obedience of those who seek Him. You are His beautiful child and part of His plan to fulfill His truth in this world.

You Are the Almighty Creator

{ GENESIS }

In the beginning, heavenly Father, You were there. Complete darkness, total silence. Emptiness. And then You opened Your mouth and declared: *Let there be light!* You broke the silence with Your almighty voice and flooded the universe with Your beautiful creations. The stars, sun, moon, and galaxies were perfectly placed at Your command. King of heaven, how can others not see your majestic wonders? How can they question Your mighty power, Your masterpiece? If only they would see Your mighty hand at work in the precise movement and placement of each piece of Your creation!

You said it was all good, and it was. But You were not finished. You created people in Your image. People with whom You, the Creator of the universe, could have a loving relationship. You wanted me. And even through the fall of man and our sinful nature, Your promise to Abraham—that he would be the father of many nations—places me in Your hands. I am Yours, and You are my God.

Your truth tells me about the promise You made Abraham: "And He took him outside and said, 'Now look toward the heavens, and count the stars, if you are able to count them.' And He said to him, 'So shall your descendants be'" (Genesis 15:5 NASB). From that moment came Your everlasting covenant:

> I will establish My covenant between Me and you and your descendants after you throughout their generations for an everlasting covenant, to be God to you and to your descendants after you. I will give to you and to your descendants after you, the land of your sojournings, all the land of Canaan, for an everlasting possession; and I will be their God (Genesis 17:7–8 NASB).

Father, this is where my journey through life begins—with You! You are my God—the God of Abraham, Isaac, and Jacob. I will follow You all the days of my life. I will also love You with an everlasting love.

. . . .

If we say we have fellowship with him while we walk
in darkness, we lie and do not practice the truth.

1 JOHN 1:6

You Are in Control

{ GENESIS }

I can't count how many times I have run ahead of You to help You out. I think that I hear Your direction, but I'm really hearing mine. And then I make a disaster out of my issue by taking control and cause more pain in my life.

You point me to Sarai. When she was finally fed up with waiting on Your promise to have a child, she essentially did what I do and took matters into her own hands. When she thought she had a better way for getting an heir, she went for it and sent Hagar to Abram's tent. O heavenly Father, help me to not be like Sarai but to trust Your timing. I know I cannot write a better story for my life than the one You have written.

Lord, when I think of Sarai's choice to take control of her situation and how she manipulated her husband and hurt Hagar, it reminds me of the impact that my choices have on the lives of others when I am not seeking You. Lord, I don't want my actions to cause pain, confusion, or hurt to anyone. And I especially don't want to hurt You!

I love how You continue to show me through Sarai that even in the midst of self-made fiascoes, You are sovereign and You are patient. You didn't turn Your back on her or Abram, but You revealed Your mighty plan. You will do the same for me. Your truth tells me,

Then God said to Abraham, "As for Sarai your wife, you shall not call her name Sarai, but Sarah shall be her name. I will bless her, and indeed I will give you a son by her. Then I will bless her, and she shall be a mother of nations; kings of peoples will come from her" (Genesis 17:15–16 NASB).

Surrendering to Your plan is not always easy. The path is difficult and uncomfortable at times. But as You did with Sarah, Abraham, and Hagar, You know the good You have planned for me if I will trust You to take me there.

O heavenly Father, I give my all to You. Forgive me for taking control of Your divine plan. My life is in Your Hands. Let Your will be done.

. . . .

He says, "Be still, and know that I am God; I will be exalted among the nations, I will be exalted in the earth."
PSALM 46:10 NIV

You Remembered Joseph

{ GENESIS }

I know I have to forgive them! It's hard to fathom that anything positive will come out of the pain I feel from my friends' disloyalty. I'm not sure what to do or how to handle my feelings! But I'm trusting You to teach me how to forgive.

Loving Father, I look to Your Word and read Joseph's example on forgiveness. His friends didn't betray him; his own brothers did! I can't fathom the agony he must've felt. It would have been so easy for him to seek revenge on his brothers when You reunited them. But Joseph kept his eyes on You. He didn't focus on his betrayal because he knew his God. He knew You had a bigger plan!

Lord, lead me with Your divine guidance as You did Joseph. Soften and fill my heart with Your love the way You did his so that I may show Your goodness, kindness, and mercy to those who have deliberately hurt me. You had a purpose for Joseph's life, and You have purpose for mine. Your truth tells me,

"You intended to harm me, but God intended it for good to accomplish what is now being done, the saving of many lives. So then, don't be afraid. I will provide for you and your children." And he reassured them and spoke kindly to them (Genesis 50:20–21 NIV).

O heavenly Father, You display Your incredible story of mercy and forgiveness, of seeing beyond the immediate situation to the eternal perspective—a story that I see again in the life of Jesus. Unlike Joseph, Jesus was perfect. Yet the people He came to save plotted against Him, cursed Him, and killed Him. Like Joseph, Jesus saw beyond the evil done to Him and looked to Your supremely sovereign hand. You had a plan—Your precious Son would save my life and the lives of Your children. Your incredible story of mercy, forgiveness, and grace! And You included me.

· · · · · · · · · · · · · · · · · · · ·

You, God, are my God, earnestly I seek you;
I thirst for you, my whole being longs for you, in a dry
and parched land where there is no water.

PSALM 63:1 NIV

You Are the Great I AM

{ EXODUS }

I come to You and lay my fears at Your feet. Why am I so afraid people will see who I really am? *If they really knew…* I think to myself, keeping my self-doubt hidden behind my insecure mask. I worry my words—my life experiences—are not worthy of what You have called me to do, Lord. Why would anyone listen to me?

You gently stop me from my thoughts, and I hear Your Spirit remind me that it is never my own personal strength that earns me a place in Your divine plan. You choose my role and then equip me with Your Spirit to bring it to pass. My work is in believing You to be who You say You are and trust You will accomplish through me whatever You have called me to do.

My almighty God, You made the answer simple when You called Moses from the burning bush. He, too, had self-doubt. I can imagine him asking You question after question, wondering why You chose him. They are the same questions I am asking You today. *What if they won't listen? What if they don't believe me? Who am I to be the one for so great a task?* You answered him:

"I am who I am." And he said, "Say this to the people of Israel: 'I am has sent me to you.'" God also said to Moses, "Say this to the people of Israel: 'The Lord, the God of your fathers, the God of Abraham, the God of Isaac, and the God of Jacob, has sent me to you.' This is my name forever, and thus I am to be remembered throughout all generations" (Exodus 3:14–15).

Your answer to Moses is the same for me. It's not who I am, it's who You are. You are the great I am and with Your Holy Spirit in me, I can dismiss any notion that I don't matter, that I can't contribute. By grasping Your truth and the knowledge of my self-existence in You, I can rise above the waves of self-doubt. I am Yours!

. . . .

Send out your light and your truth; let them lead me;
let them bring me to your holy hill and to your dwelling!
Psalm 43:3

You Clear My Path

{ EXODUS }

It's difficult to see Your perfect plan in my life when I feel lost about what to do or how to resolve my current situation. But my hope is in You! O heavenly Father, You never cease clearing Your righteous path for Your children.

Father, I bow my knees in Your presence and long to hear Your voice—like Moses heard You in the burning bush. When I close my eyes and think about him and the Israelites, who had been in slavery for over four hundred years, I feel guilty when I focus on my feelings of hopelessness. There is no comparison to what they must have felt! You, the great I AM, heard their cries and pulled them out of their misery when they hungered for Your guidance and hope. O Lord, I hunger too.

Now as I sit in Your presence and meditate on Your Word, You speak to my heart and tell me that Your truth doesn't change. You hear me, Lord, like You heard them. And it is Your almighty hand that will lift me out of my sufferings. Just as You showed Moses Your identity in the desert, You displayed Your saving power to Your people and to the observing Egyptians—and to me. You knew I would need lessons like this all these years later.

Plague after plague unleashed a torrent of consequences, each one aimed at dethroning the many gods the Egyptians worshiped. I cannot imagine that kind of devastation. But even though Egypt was stripped of almost everything, You made sure Your people stood by unharmed, ready for freedom. You were there in the center of it all. Hope arrived.

The power to save Your people resided only in You: the God of Abraham, Isaac, and Jacob. The same power that saves me. Thank You, Lord, that in Egypt a new relationship was born and a covenant was established that has been passed along to me. Your truth tells me,

> Then Moses went up to God, and the LORD called to him from the mountain and said, "This is what you are to say to the descendants of Jacob and what you are to tell the people of Israel: 'You yourselves have seen what I did to Egypt, and how I carried you on eagles' wings and brought you to myself. Now if you obey me fully and keep my covenant, then out of all nations you will be my treasured possession'" (Exodus 19:3–5 NIV).

Your promises never cease. I am Your treasured possession—Your child. And You will carry me on eagles' wings, guide me, and bring me into Your protective arms.

. . . .

The LORD is good to those who wait for him,
to the soul who seeks him.
LAMENTATIONS 3:25

You Are Holy

{ LEVITICUS }

Lord of all creation, I fall to my knees when I hear You tell me for the first time that You are holy! All-powerful God, there is no one above You. And You have set me apart and called me to be holy. "Thus you are to be holy to Me, for I the Lord am holy; and I have set you apart from the peoples to be Mine" (Leviticus 20:26 NASB). How can I? I am a sinner! Is this even possible?

You gently raise me up and unveil a blueprint of Your amazing grace, knowing that I could never be holy under the law. It's impossible for me, for I am an unrighteous sinner. Your mighty Word reveals that the blood sacrifice of a lamb was a glimpse of what was to come—Your perfect Son, Jesus. The Son of God entered our world, not to destroy the law but to fulfill it. He lived the righteous life that I can never live. He was the perfect sacrificial Lamb who offered up His own life so that I could become spotless. Through His sacrifice, His righteousness, I am covered by His blood. I am cleansed. I am holy.

Lord, thank You for showing me that the law was given through Moses, but Your grace was given through Your precious Son, Jesus. Your truth tells me,

By that will, we have been made holy through the sacrifice of the body of Jesus Christ once for all (Hebrews 10:10 NIV).

It is Jesus Christ alone who gives me the holiness that I need to stand before You. Lord, I praise Your holy name, for I am holy because You are holy.

. . . .

I will also praise You with a harp,
even Your truth, O my God;
to You I will sing praises with the lyre,
O Holy One of Israel.
PSALM 71:22 NASB

You Are Lifted Up

Why is it that I praise and seek You only in the good times but complain when things aren't going *my* way? I feel like I'm barely out of Egypt, like the Israelites grumbling against You, God, for taking me out of my comfort zone and into unknown desert, only to struggle with my current situation or to be bitten by the snakes of this world. What is it that You are trying to teach me? I can't find contentment with where I am!

How quickly You show me that if I continue grumbling and walking in my disobedience, the metaphorical serpents of this world will bite me. My eyes are not seeking the One You lifted up to give me an abundant life—eternal life. I've been consumed, living in the moment and living my way. Your truth tells me,

Then the LORD sent fiery serpents among the people, and they bit the people, so that many people of Israel died. And the people came to Moses and said, "We have sinned, for we have spoken against the LORD and against you. Pray to the LORD that he take away the serpents from us." So Moses prayed for the people.

And the LORD said to Moses, "Make a fiery serpent and set it on a pole, and everyone who is bitten, when he sees it, shall live." So Moses made a bronze serpent and set it on a pole. And if a serpent bit anyone, he would look up at the bronze serpent and live (Numbers 21:6–9).

Your Son was lifted up on the cross to die so I could be with You forever. And when I keep my eyes looking up to You, Jesus, I see truth. I live! Your truth tells me, "And as Moses lifted up the serpent in the wilderness, so must the Son of Man be lifted up, that whoever believes in him may have eternal life" (John 3:14–15). My Savior, I lift my arms to worship You and trust You in my unknown desert!

. . . .

The LORD looks down from heaven on the children of man,
to see if there are any who understand, who seek after God.
PSALM 14:2

You Bless Me

{ DEUTERONOMY }

It's unbelievable to think that I am the apple of Your eye!
That You, almighty God, who called Abraham, Isaac, Jacob
—who lifted up Moses to deliver Your chosen Israel from
Egypt—would bless me! I think about the Israelites' journey
and what it was like. They were so close to the promised land.
They could see it, but some would not be allowed to enter
because of their disobedience. Did they miss out on Your
blessings? Would I have been one of those who disobeyed You?

Even today life offers plenty of distractions and opportunities for me to either trust or disobey Your commands. The
lure of the false gods and idols of this world can tempt anyone
and cause them to stumble. But You have given me Your Word
and Your promises to guide me through my wilderness. Your
truth tells me,

> If you obey the commandments of the LORD your
> God that I command you today, by loving the LORD
> your God, by walking in his ways, and by keeping his
> commandments and his statutes and his rules, then
> you shall live and multiply, and the LORD your God

will bless you in the land that you are entering to take possession of it (Deuteronomy 30:16).

Lord, You know that not much has changed in today's world. Many people are still lost in the desert. They don't know that they, too, are the apple of Your eye, that they are chosen. You still pour out overflowing blessings for those who seek to know Your ways, to love You and to know truth in Jesus. "You are a chosen people, a royal priesthood, a holy nation, God's special possession, that you may declare the praises of him who called you out of darkness into his wonderful light" (1 Peter 2:9 NIV). O Father, there is no greater blessing.

. . . .

From there you will seek the Lord your God
and you will find him, if you search after him
with all your heart and with all your soul.
Deuteronomy 4:29

You Fight My Battles

Be strong and courageous! I hear Your words, mighty God, that You spoke to Joshua. You are the same God today that You were then, but my faith has been shaken and I feel that I'm falling under the pressure. Though I may never wage war in foreign lands like Joshua, life itself is filled with battles bigger than I can handle on my own.

I think about Your presence in Joshua's life and how he witnessed Your authority. He saw You deliver Your chosen people in Egypt and watched You provide all they needed in the desert. He was there when You blessed them from the mountaintop and disciplined them in the valley below. O Lord, I long to see Your sovereignty in everything that surrounds me, but I feel so weak when I am confronted by trials of this world.

Heavenly Father, I ponder Your words to Joshua. It was Your power—not his—that equipped him to conquer his enemies. You gave him strength. That same power lives within me. You fought his battles, and now I lay mine at Your feet.

Your Holy Spirit tells me to be strong and courageous— You are near and will shelter me from the storm. You are the same God who gave Joshua victory in the promised land, and

You will do the same for me. I am never alone. Your truth tells me,

> "Have I not commanded you? Be strong and courageous. Do not be frightened, and do not be dismayed, for the LORD your God is with you wherever you go" (Joshua 1:9).

In Your strength, there is nothing I can't do. Lord, open my eyes day by day to see that You have me in Your mighty arms. Knowing that You are by my side gives me courage and strength to serve You in truth all the days of my life.

. . . .

Now, therefore, fear the LORD
and serve Him in sincerity and truth.
JOSHUA 24:14 NASB

You Are My Judge

How could anyone forget You? How could Your chosen people not seek Your guidance after the way You manifested Your power and glory in delivering them from Egypt and establishing them in the land You promised them? You fought their battles. You provided every need. You gave them light in the darkness.

Lord, I think about how it didn't take long after the death of Joshua for the Israelites to reject You and Your everlasting covenant. They lived as though they were of the world, worshipping other gods and idols with no direction. But You did not forget them when You heard their groans. And You lifted up judges to deliver them from their enemies. When they listened to You, they prospered. When they didn't, they fell.

Your truth tells me,

> Whenever the LORD raised up judges for them, the LORD was with the judge, and he saved them from the hand of their enemies all the days of the judge. For the LORD was moved to pity by their groaning because of those who afflicted and oppressed them (Judges 2:18).

Abba Father, it's only in seeking You and Your Word daily that I am kept from following in their footsteps. The world is full of false gods and idols that lure me to forget Your greatness. It pierces my heart to think that there are times in my life that I am misled. You can easily wipe my rebellious self from Your sight when I ignore Your hand at work in every aspect of my life. But You don't. You continue loving and shaping me into the person You've called me to be.

You are my ultimate Judge—my Father—a God of patience, love, and faithfulness. I don't deserve Your love, but You offer it to me with open arms because I belong to You. My ears long to hear Your voice so that I may stand on steady ground and not fall from Your ways.

. . . .

My people, hear my teaching; listen to the words of my mouth. I will open my mouth with a parable; I will utter hidden things, things from of old—things we have heard and known, things our ancestors have told us. We will not hide them from their descendants; we will tell the next generation the praiseworthy deeds of the LORD, his power, and the wonders he has done.

PSALM 78:1–4 NIV

You Are with Me

{ RUTH }

Throughout my life I've always felt like an outsider—constantly trying to find a place where I belong. Will I ever find it?

You, dear Lord, point me to the book of Ruth. Naomi must have felt that way too when severe famine drove her and her husband, Mahlon, and their two sons out of Israel to the foreign land of Moab. Her dreams were shattered when her husband and sons suddenly died. How my heart aches for her, thinking about the panic she must have felt living in the midst of a heathen culture without her husband's provision. But You, sovereign Father, knew that her feelings of abandonment were temporary and that her bitter grief would soon turn to joy. What love You displayed as You placed her devoted, widowed daughter-in-law, Ruth, by her side as the two journeyed back home to Bethlehem. Your almighty plan was about to unfold.

Father, forgive me when I focus on my shattered dreams like Naomi and weep bitter tears when I feel utterly forgotten and all alone. You remind me that, because Your Spirit lives within me, I am never alone. You provide me with encouragement through those You've placed in my life.

O Father, how wonderful to see how You cared for Naomi in ways she could never have dreamed—placing Boaz, a kinsman-redeemer, in her life to marry Ruth and usher her back into hope. Through Boaz and Ruth's love and loyalty, You birthed a line of descendants leading to Your precious Son, Jesus Himself.

Thank You for choosing the broken and rewarding those who seek You—who yield to Your lead, using every moment in their lives to make an outcome designed for Your glory and our good. Thank You for choosing me. Your truth tells me,

May the LORD reward your work, and your wages be full from the LORD, the God of Israel, under whose wings you have come to seek refuge (Ruth 2:12 NASB).

. . . .

In him you also, when you heard the word of truth,
the gospel of your salvation, and believed in him,
were sealed with the promised Holy Spirit.
EPHESIANS 1:13

You Heard Naomi's Cry

{ RUTH }

Lord, why couldn't my loved one stay a little longer? Will my days get easier and will my heart heal from the sting of death?

Father, Your Word unveils Your amazing love for me as I study the book of Ruth. Naomi's pain after the death of her husband and two sons must have been unbearable. It would've been so easy for her to think You had abandoned her. But You, almighty God, had Naomi in Your hands and stood in the midst of Naomi's chaos—orchestrating a great love story that would redeem us all, that would redeem me!

Naomi knew her God. She heard about Your provision while living in a foreign country and arose! Her story is compelling:

> Then she arose with her daughters-in-law to return from the country of Moab, for she had heard in the fields of Moab that the LORD had visited his people and given them food. So she set out from the place where she was with her two daughters-in-law, and they went on the way to return to the land of Judah (Ruth 1:6–7).

You had not forgotten Your people in Judah despite their disobedience. Naomi, along with her daughter-in-law Ruth, was going home to the place where she belonged—Judah. She belonged to You, and You had a plan to redeem her! And through her lineage, Your precious Son, Jesus, was born— the kinsman-redeemer who redeemed us all.

What an awesome love story of Your sovereignty and abiding love. You thought of me when You redeemed Naomi. My heart overflows with joy that You have claimed me as Your own. I am Yours. And You are mine.

. . . .

May all who seek you rejoice and be glad in you!
May those who love your salvation say evermore, "God is great!"
PSALM 70:4

You Hear My Prayers

{ 1 SAMUEL }

You are more precious than anything else on this earth. Nothing compares to Your love. I pray that I will learn to relinquish my grasp on the things of this world that You have given me. I think of Hannah and how she prayed fervently for You to grant her a child. "For this child I prayed, and the LORD has granted me my petition that I made to him. Therefore I have lent him to the LORD. As long as he lives, he is lent to the LORD" (1 Samuel 1:27–28).

Heavenly Father, I can't imagine how Hannah felt the day she left her young son, Samuel, at the tabernacle—letting go of the one thing she had desired her entire life. I'm not sure if I could've done the same. Perhaps that's why You reveal Hannah's unshakable faith. Little did she know that You would raise up her firstborn son to become the spiritual leader of Israel and anoint Your first two kings, Saul and David, to rule Your chosen people.

Lord, forgive me when I clutch too tightly what I think is mine. I learn from Your Word that Hannah turned to You in need and You answered her prayer. She praised and thanked You and kept an open hand with Your blessing, allowing even her deepest desire to be given away for Your glory. And

You blessed her even more. I believe You will do the same for me.

This makes me think of how You, too, opened Your hand and gave Your one and only Son to us, that through Jesus we might have eternal life with You. Your truth tells me,

Jesus said to her, "I am the resurrection and the life. The one who believes in me will live, even though they die; and whoever lives by believing in me will never die. Do you believe this?" (John 11:25–26 NIV).

Yes, I believe! And I let go of everything and raise my arms to You and give You all my praise.

. . . .

Seek first the kingdom of God and his righteousness,
and all these things will be added to you.
MATTHEW 6:33

You Are the King of Kings

{ 1 SAMUEL }

You had told them they were chosen—Your own precious people, called out to be distinctly faithful to You. Called to be blessed beyond their wildest dreams.

But the Israelites said no. No to Your intimate leadership. No to Your invitation to commune with You. No to Your provision for love and security. Instead of believing and trusting You as their good and sovereign Lord, they wanted to grasp the power themselves. Turning to the world's ways, they rejected Your true way to life. They wanted a king like the other nations. How could they not want You as King?

Heavenly King, Your heart must have broken when Your children rejected You—especially after all that You had done for them. It wasn't enough. They still desired more. They chose to be led by the world.

Lord, this makes me reflect on my own self-centered attitude. I can be the same way as the Israelites! When I don't seek You, I look to my own ability and power to make choices in my life. O Father, forgive me! I don't want to break Your heart!

You, the Almighty, take Your seat center stage and You reign on Your throne. I lift up my eyes to You. You have given me eternal life through Jesus, the King of kings and Lord of lords who has authority over all. I belong to You. Your truth tells me,

> For the sake of his great name the Lord will not reject
> his people, because the Lord was pleased to make you
> his own (1 Samuel 12:22 NIV).

I no longer want to break Your heart. Lead me, God, in all that I do. I long to be covered by Your power and grace. I say yes to You, the King of kings, for the rest of my life.

. . . .

With my whole heart I seek you;
let me not wander from your commandments!
PSALM 119:10

You Keep Me Humble

How could someone so close to You from the start spiral down a wrong path and fall out of Your favor?

I think of King Saul—Your first chosen king of Israel. At first he seemed the perfect choice. You gave him a peaceful reign. However, it didn't last long. His disobedience to Your commands and then his attempt to cover up his transgressions by lying to Samuel—to You—made it impossible for him to lead. He didn't put You first in His life. It was all about him. His destructive pride destroyed his reign. Lord, his story opens my eyes to my own pride. There are times when I think it's all about me and I neglect to put You first in my life.

Lord, I know from Your Word that there are consequences to my prideful choices. You withdrew Your Spirit from Saul and chose a humble shepherd boy, David, to take his place. Your truth tells me,

> Samuel said to Saul, "You have done foolishly. You have not kept the command of the LORD your God, with which he commanded you. For then the LORD would have established your kingdom over Israel forever. But now your kingdom shall not continue.

The LORD has sought out a man after his own heart, and the LORD has commanded him to be prince over his people, because you have not kept what the LORD commanded you" (1 Samuel 13:13–14).

You teach me how to surrender to Your almighty power as I read that King Saul chased David like a madman, trying to kill him for his popularity and growing power. Yet in honor to You and Your established authority, David humbly refused to return harm to Saul, even when he had ample opportunity.

Later, You lifted David up as king. This makes me think of Jesus at the cross. He could've stopped those who were trying to kill Him, but He didn't. Instead, He humbled Himself and died on the cross. He thought of me and all humanity, not Himself. He came to serve, not to be served.

O King of kings, I humbly fall on my knees and worship You—and You only. Lord, You know if I don't seek You and keep my eyes focused on Your Word, pride will creep into my heart. O heavenly Father, let it never happen! Don't let me think that I am worthy of praise. I never want to forget that You are sovereign. You alone rule over all creation. You alone are worthy of praise!

· · · · · · · · · · · · · · · · · · · ·

It is not good to eat much honey,
nor is it glorious to seek one's own glory.
PROVERBS 25:27

You Restore My Life

{ 2 SAMUEL }

Can a person truly love You and pursue Your glory, and still seriously sin? Can such a person be forgiven and restored? What about me? Would You turn Your back on me if I failed You?

I come to You in the stillness of the night, searching Your Word. I love how You chose David and anointed him king of Israel. He was a man after Your own heart. He loved you and bravely trusted You for protection. He stood firmly on Your truth. No one questioned his devotion—David's heart belonged to You. Oh, how I long to live at that level of devotion, but I keep making mistakes.

You, gracious God, show me that David took his eyes off You and turned from Your commands when he saw Bathsheba. David wanted her as his own, knowing it was wrong. Before long, he was covering sin with sin, thinking he could hide it from everyone, including You. But You exposed it:

Why have you despised the word of the LORD, to do what is evil in his sight? You have struck down Uriah the Hittite with the sword and have taken his wife to be your wife and have killed him with the sword of the Ammonites (2 Samuel 12:9).

O Lord, David, who loved You with all of his heart, failed You miserably. I am in good company. I learn that in his deep sorrow, he turned back to seek Your mercy and compassion. David didn't deny his sin or excuse it—he simply repented. Deeply and truly, He turned to You and admitted everything. You, gracious God, granted forgiveness and full reconciliation. You will do the same for me.

Father, forgive me when I try to hide my sins from You. Your truth tells me, "Nothing in all creation is hidden from God's sight. Everything is uncovered and laid bare before the eyes of him to whom we must give account" (Hebrews 4:13 NIV). Though there will be many days when I will fall even as a redeemed believer, I realize that when I come to You with a broken and contrite heart, You will draw me back through the saving blood of Jesus. I am forgiven, Your child after Your own heart.

· · · · · · · · · · · · · · · · · · ·

He restores my soul. He leads me in paths
of righteousness for his name's sake.
PSALM 23:3

You Silence the Unbelievers

{ 1 KINGS }

Your critics are everywhere. My faith is constantly challenged by those who don't believe in Your sovereignty. Even so, almighty God, I stand on solid ground because I know who You are—You are my God, the only true God. It is You whom I seek daily. It breaks my heart that unbelievers are seeking idols that will never bring them fulfillment.

I remember Elijah's challenge to the Israelites. When he questioned them about You, they said nothing. They wanted it both ways: to worship hundreds of idols and You at the same time. So much like the world today. We have become silent regarding Your supreme power. But You displayed Your sovereignty when Your faithful prophet drew a sharp contrast between the worship of You and that of Baal.

Your truth tells me,

"Answer me, O Lord, answer me, that this people may know that You, O Lord, are God, and that You have turned their heart back again." Then the fire of the Lord fell and consumed the burnt offering and the wood and the stones and the dust, and licked up the water that was in the trench. When all the people saw it, they fell on their faces; and they said, "The LORD, He is God; the LORD, He is God" (1 Kings 18:37–39 NASB).

In Your mercy, You allowed the Israelites to see with their eyes what their hearts should have known all along: You alone are God.

You have proven Your sovereignty throughout history and through Your Word. And today, You've chosen me to silence Your critics by revealing Your Spirit, the light and power that lives within me. You are my God. I pray that I will never be silent in sharing Your truth.

. . . .

Elijah went before the people and said,
"How long will you waver between two opinions?
If the LORD is God, follow him; but if Baal is God, follow him."
But the people said nothing.
1 KINGS 18:21 NIV

You Know My Future

Horoscopes. Magic 8-Balls. Ouija boards. Psychics. Lord, our society deceives us into believing these are simple entertainments, but that's a lie! People all over the world turn to whatever or whomever they can to find out what their future holds. *Is it written in the stars or the palm of their hand?* If they only knew the truth—it's not in their hand but Yours! You, God, are the only one who holds our future in Your hands.

I wonder about Ahaziah, Israel's king. He found himself in a similar predicament when he fell through the lattice in his house and was injured. He did what it seemed everybody else around him did—he sent his messengers to call on psychic powers to find out his fate.

Dear Lord, protect my heart from such deception! In Ahaziah's day, they called on Baal-Zebub, the god of Ekron. Though we use different names today, divination still has the same effect on You, God. You hate it. And You made Ahaziah's future clear through Elijah's response to his messengers. Your truth tells me,

The angel of the LORD said to Elijah the Tishbite, "Go up and meet the messengers of the king of

Samaria and ask them, 'Is it because there is no God in Israel that you are going off to consult Baal-Zebub, the god of Ekron?' Therefore this is what the LORD says: 'You will not leave the bed you are lying on. You will certainly die!'" (2 Kings 1:3–4 NIV).

All-powerful God, it's only Your revealed Word that I can rely upon for unfailing wisdom and guidance. I don't need to seek information about my future from the world. I have Jesus, and through Him, I have access to Your throne. You hear and answer my prayers—You alone. You are sovereign, and I trust You with my life. I trust You with my unknowns.

. . . .

Do not turn to mediums or necromancers;
do not seek them out, and so make yourselves
unclean by them: I am the LORD your God.
LEVITICUS 19:31

You Cleanse Prideful Hearts

{ 2 KINGS }

You bring meaning to my life when I feel insignificant. You, Father, give the example of a young Israelite who was stolen from her family and home, and made a slave to the commander of the army of Israel's enemy, the Arameans. Her name isn't even mentioned in Scripture. But You touched her heart, then used to touch the heart of her master—a Gentile named Naaman. He desperately needed help, and she was quick to tell him about the God who could heal him. You, Jehovah-Rapha! Lord, I want to be like her. She didn't think twice about sharing her God with her enemy.

There was a roadblock, however. You, sovereign God, knew his prideful heart! After arriving in Israel, Naaman expected a grand greeting from Your prophet. Instead, when he was given simple instructions on how to lose the leprosy, Naaman became furious. I wonder if he was thinking, *Doesn't Elisha know how important I am?* His servants had to redirect his prideful thinking. Lord, You surrounded him with humble servants who showed him truth. Surround me with people like that.

Naaman had a choice to make—the same choice I have:

obey and believe or live with a prideful heart. He chose You. I choose You. He listened, was completely healed, and became Your servant.

> Then Naaman and all his attendants went back to the man of God. He stood before him and said, "Now I know that there is no God in all the world except in Israel. So please accept a gift from your servant (2 Kings 5:15 NIV).

Lord, Naaman's healing from leprosy is a wonderful picture of our salvation from sin—freely given by Your grace in response to faith. And it's an illustration of what You would later do in the ministry of Your Son and His church—reaching the Jews and the Gentiles. You reached me! Your truth tells me that salvation cannot be bought or earned, "for by grace you have been saved through faith. And this is not your own doing; it is the gift of God, not a result of works, so that no one may boast" (Ephesians 2:8–9).

Her name was unknown, but her impact was powerful. Lord, use my unknown name too! I want to be Your servant and tell others about Your truth.

. . . .

In the pride of his face the wicked does not seek him;
all his thoughts are, "There is no God."
PSALM 10:4

Your Records Are True

{ 1 CHRONICLES }

When will I learn that my plans are not Your plans? That my way is not Your way? It's sometimes difficult for me to see Your hand at work in my life, especially when my wait is long. Even though Your methods are often mysterious and far different from what I can conceive, I know You are faithful.

Lord, I've always wondered why You meticulously recorded the events and names of people that seem so insignificant compared to what is going on in my life. But as I dig deeper into Your Word, You touch my heart and I begin to understand. You were thinking about me. You, who are all-knowing, want me to seek You and watch Your amazing plan and purpose unfold. Your truth tells me, "He remembers his covenant forever, the promise he made, for a thousand generations" (1 Chronicles 16:15 NIV).

I see myself in Your blueprint as You teach me that the people of Israel faced many trials, enjoyed life, and experienced peace through the circumstances and people You placed in their lives. I am astonished to discover that You chose a lowly shepherd boy to become Israel's powerful king and established his throne forever, though the people didn't really understand what You were doing.

Little did they know—and little did I know until now—that though David's victorious reign prospered in his affection for You and truth, You were paving the way for another king from David's ancestry whose power and rule would never end. Jesus. O Father God, Your records of the events and names of Your people lead to You. Your records show me the lineage: "The record of the genealogy of Jesus the Messiah, the son of David, the son of Abraham" (Matthew 1:1 NASB). Through Your Son—Jesus, born of David's royal line from the tribe of Judah—You, God, would finally resolve Your covenant promise of redemption. Opening wide the gates of salvation to every Jewish and Gentile soul that receives Him, You've established eternal hope for all of Your people from every tribe and nation. You have established eternal hope and life for me!

· · · · · · · · · · · · · · · · · ·

Sing to Him, sing praises to Him; speak of all His wonders.
Glory in His holy name; let the heart of those who seek
the LORD be glad. Seek the LORD and His strength;
seek His face continually.
1 CHRONICLES 16:9–11 NASB

You Are the Mighty God Who Saves

{ 2 CHRONICLES }

Lord, as I cry out to You in prayer, I lift my hands in desperation for Your saving hand in my time of distress. I reflect on Your Word and the time Your people in Judah were in trouble and knew it. A vast army was bearing down on them, poised to destroy them. It was just a matter of time. But You were there! You were there then, and I know You are with me now.

Father, You knew the people of Judah were powerless to defeat their enemies. Just like I feel powerless now. I love how they positioned themselves before You, under King Jehoshaphat's lead, and joined together in prayer before You. Standing as one under Your sovereign gaze, they looked to You and asked for help: "Our God, will you not judge them? For we have no power to face this vast army that is attacking us. We do not know what to do, but our eyes are on you" (2 Chronicles 20:12 NIV).

With expectant hope, they hid themselves in Your power, trusting that You would save them. And You did! O God, I long to hide myself in Your power, knowing You will save me!

Roused by compassion and intense love for Your people, You encouraged them to take heart. Then You told them to step out in faith—to literally walk out and face their enemies and watch what You would do. You turned their enemies against one another until they were destroyed. I hear Your Spirit telling me to do the same today.

Where do I turn when I face impossible odds? I turn to You, Lord! Your truth tells me,

> This is what the LORD says to you: "Do not be afraid or discouraged because of this vast army. For the battle is not yours, but God's" (2 Chronicles 20:15 NIV).

I, too, will face my enemies head-on and rest knowing the battle is Yours, not mine. You are the mighty God who saves!

. . . .

The people of Judah came together to seek help from the LORD;
indeed, they came from every town in Judah to seek him.
2 CHRONICLES 20:4 NIV

You Welcome Me Home

{ EZRA }

They had lost it all. Having crossed the Jordan to claim the land You promised them, Israel had once enjoyed abundant blessing from You, who called them Your own people. But time and time again, they abandoned the truth for temporary pleasures! Lord, times haven't changed much. Even today we, the body of Christ, are so quick to turn from You for the things of this world that will never make us happy.

Why can't we grasp Your heart? Your incredible compassion? Your relentless determination to bless Your people and be with us despite our infidelity? You lay it in front of me in the book of Ezra, when Your people began to see the miracle.

It doesn't surprise me that You touched the heart of the king of Persia and he suddenly commanded that Your temple in Jerusalem be rebuilt, a project funded by his own treasury. I'm captivated by Your ways and how You stirred the spirits of Your people from all over to come restore what had been lost.

Even while under foreign rule, You united Your people once more through Your call to worship. Just as their bodies had journeyed from distant places back to home, so had their hearts. The remnant had come full circle, and the center was You, God. And it still is.

The same miracle happens for every remorseful child of Yours. There's no place so far from home that we can't return to You. Your truth tells me how You turned the heart of a foreign king to lead Your chosen people home:

> Now these were the people of the province who came up out of the captivity of those exiles whom Nebuchadnezzar the king of Babylon had carried captive to Babylonia. They returned to Jerusalem and Judah, each to his own town (Ezra 2:1).

You welcomed Your children home!

Lord, You always embrace me back with Your love, forgiveness, and fellowship blazing when I repent and turn my face fully toward You. I do, and Your glory surrounds me.

. . . .

Then the family heads of Judah and Benjamin,
and the priests and Levites—everyone whose heart
God had moved—prepared to go up and build
the house of the LORD in Jerusalem.

EZRA 1:5 NIV

You Listen

{ NEHEMIAH }

O heavenly Father, great and awesome God, You hear my prayers and give me strength in my time of need. The task in front of me is too difficult.

Your words in the book of Nehemiah give me a glimpse into how essential faith and prayer are to You. I think of Nehemiah, a layman and a cupbearer to a foreign king. His heart was heavy because he longed to lead the Jews who had returned to Jerusalem in rebuilding the wall. I imagine he knew it would be a daunting, strenuous task, to be sure, because the old wall still lay on the ground in a heap of useless rubble. But what was the first thing he did? He prayed.

Lord, Nehemiah's situation is a perfect example of what I should do before I accomplish or consider anything. Pray. He knew that You were faithful to Your covenant and You alone could provide the strength they needed for success. Your truth tells me,

O LORD God of heaven, the great and awesome God who keeps covenant and steadfast love with those who love him and keep his commandments, let your ear be attentive and your eyes open, to hear the prayer of your servant that I now pray before you day and night for the people of Israel your servants, confessing the sins of the people of Israel, which we have sinned against you. Even I and my father's house have sinned (Nehemiah 1:5–6).

Father, You listened to Nehemiah and answered his prayers. My heart rejoices that You gave him wisdom to lead and protect Your people. They took up arms to protect what belonged to them and what You called them to do.

You, Lord, do the same for me! Because You are faithful to Your covenant and to those who love You, You hear my prayers. And when the walls of my life are falling down all around me, You give me strength and wisdom. You rebuild and restore me.

• • • • • • • • • • • • • • • • • • • •

When you are in distress and all these things have come upon you, in the latter days you will return to the LORD your God and listen to His voice. For the LORD your God is a compassionate God; He will not fail you nor destroy you nor forget the covenant with your fathers which He swore to them.

DEUTERONOMY 4:30–31 NASB

You Call Me in Times Such as These

{ ESTHER }

Even in the stillness of night when I don't feel Your presence, I know You are still there. Although Your name was never mentioned in the book of Esther, You, God, chose her—an orphaned Jewish girl—and raised her up to be royalty. Out of all the women in Persia, she was crowned queen. You knew that disaster was looming over Your people. But You, almighty King, held the outcome in Your sovereign hand.

Even when I can't see You at work, You reveal to me that You are orchestrating Your divine plan. Esther rose from obscurity to one of the most powerful positions possible—to save Your beloved people. For such a time as this, she trusted You for guidance:

> For if you keep silent at this time, relief and deliverance will rise for the Jews from another place, but you and your father's house will perish. And who knows whether you have not come to the kingdom for such a time as this? (Esther 4:14).

Sovereign Lord, You are all-knowing. Your plans are perfect. "Oh, the depth of the riches and wisdom and knowledge of God! How unsearchable are his judgments and how inscrutable his ways! 'For who has known the mind of the Lord, or who has been his counselor?' 'Or who has given a gift to him that he might be repaid?' For from him and through him and to him are all things. To him be glory forever. Amen" (Romans 11:33–36).

So when I face insurmountable odds, I know that You are near. You have not left me as an orphan but have chosen me to be Your child—Your royalty. May I always seek Your guidance and wisdom in times such as these.

. . . .

Whoever diligently seeks good seeks favor,
but evil comes to him who searches for it.
Proverbs 11:27

50

You Allow It to Happen

{ JOB }

I had it all—the perfect life. And then it was gone. Lord, I don't understand why You let my life take such a drastic turn. I've loved You most my life. I've followed You faithfully. How could this happen?

As I wonder, Your Word speaks to me. Job had it all—wealth, fame, a beautiful family—and he followed You with his whole heart. His devout faith had Your attention—and Satan's too. But Satan wasn't convinced that his faith was real. He felt certain that Job's devotion was a direct result of Your blessing. I question why You would allow Satan to test him. Why would You remove all of his blessings?

But then You answer my questions. You knew Job's heart; it belonged to You. Job went from having it all to having nothing at all, nothing except You—the God who gives and takes away. I admire Job for remaining firm in his faith, even while he struggled with You over how he was being treated. In the end, his friends were silenced. Satan was silenced. Job was silenced. You spoke and displayed Your power and strength. You proclaimed Your sovereignty! "Where were you when I laid the foundations of the earth? Tell Me if you have understanding" (Job 38:4 NASB).

Sometimes it takes a test, even to the point of losing everything I hold dear in this life, to determine where my true affections lie. Testing my faith isn't for You. It's to prove that my faith in You is real. Your truth tells me,

In this you rejoice, though now for a little while, if necessary, you have been grieved by various trials, so that the tested genuineness of your faith—more precious than gold that perishes though it is tested by fire—may be found to result in praise and glory and honor at the revelation of Jesus Christ (1 Peter 1:6–7).

Lord, no matter what trials I face or what drastic turns my life takes, I will seek You and run to Your loving arms.

. . . .

Seek the LORD, and His strength; seek His face continually.
PSALM 105:4 NASB

You Are Lord of All

Heavenly Father, sometimes I take Your holiness for granted, and I dash off a prayer here and there, asking for this or that while I am on the run. When I stop my daily activities long enough to look up to You, the moment is often filled with rambling words or scrambled thoughts that I hope You will understand as prayer.

But the psalmist reminds me that coming before You, acknowledging You as Lord of all creation, is not something I am to do lightly or irreverently. O almighty God, my Father, You are my Rock, my strength, and You bless me abundantly, more than I deserve. I am extremely sorry that I neglect spending time with You and giving You praise for everything You do in my life. Your truth tells me,

> The LORD reigns, let the nations tremble; he sits enthroned between the cherubim, let the earth shake. Great is the LORD in Zion; he is exalted over all the nations. Let them praise your great and awesome name—he is holy (Psalm 99:1–3 NIV).

I acknowledge Your authority and that Your plan for all of eternity is unfolding. I am left amazed; I fall on my face before You, the Holy One, who controls it all. Forgive me, Lord. I fall silent because of Your greatness, overwhelmed by the power of Your mercy. What amazing grace, that You have opened the door to Your holy presence through Your Son, my Savior, Jesus.

· · · · · · · · · · · · · · · · · · · ·

Who is God, but the Lord? And who is a rock,
except our God?—the God who equipped me with strength
and made my way blameless. He made my feet like the feet
of a deer and set me secure on the heights.

Psalm 18:31–33

You Created Me

{ PSALMS }

You were there the moment my child was born. Tears of joy streamed from my eyes as I held my son in my arms. I thought about You, and I wondered how anyone could not believe in Your miracle of life.

Lord, Your amazing power of creation is everywhere. A power like no other. When I open my Bible, You reveal Your sovereignty, strength, and purpose from the beginning to the end, from Genesis to Revelation. I marvel at how You work in minute detail, creating Your world and preparing Your children—child by child—to do extraordinary feats to display Your truth and promises.

Lord, as I read David's words in the book of Psalms, I realize that I am a miracle and a part of Your plan. You knew me before I existed, and I can only imagine the joy You must have felt the day I was born. Your truth tells me,

For you formed my inward parts; you knitted me together in my mother's womb. I praise you, for I am fearfully and wonderfully made. Wonderful are your works; my soul knows it very well. My frame was not hidden from you, when I was being made in secret, intricately woven in the depths of the earth. Your eyes saw my unformed substance; in your book were written, every one of them, the days that were formed for me, when as yet there was none of them (Psalm 139:13–16).

Father, I love You with all of my heart, and I seek Your guidance in my life every day. I pray that You will use my life to do extraordinary feats to reveal Your grace and forgiveness to others.

Thank You for loving and blessing me with unique and special gifts that only I can share with the world. You created me like no other. I am one of a kind, and I belong to You. I am Your child.

. . . .

With all my heart I have sought You; do not let me wander
from Your commandments. Your word I have treasured
in my heart, that I may not sin against You.
PSALM 119:10–11 NASB

You Are Wisdom

{ PROVERBS }

In a world of global technology, everything is at my fingertips. It's all only a click away. But You, God, are the source of all wisdom. Why do people look to a broken world for life's meaning and not to You?

I think of Solomon in the book of Proverbs. More than anything, he wanted wisdom. So over riches, fame, and power, he asked You for understanding. You, God, were very pleased with his request. And You gave it freely! But Your generosity doesn't stop with him. You promise all believers—You promise me—that You will gladly give Your wisdom to anyone who asks for it. Your truth tells me,

> Get wisdom; get insight; do not forget, and do not turn away from the words of my mouth (Proverbs 4:5).

You are the source of all wisdom, and the world is not! When I seek You for direction for my life, a beautiful miracle happens: I begin to walk and live in truth. And truth applied to life in all my daily thoughts and details leads to real wisdom. It leads to peace.

As I meditate on the Proverbs, I reflect on Your nature, the effects of sin, and my need for truth in my daily life. You give me a deeper understanding of who You are. You are omniscient. You are wisdom! And to become wise is to draw closer to You, from whom wisdom comes. It's Your gift to guide me through this broken world!

Heavenly Father, learning from You becomes my link to greater understanding—not only of how and why the world works as it does, but also how You are at work behind it, using all You have made for Your glory. It is all for Your glory!

. . . .

Let your heart hold fast my words;
keep my commandments, and live.
PROVERBS 4:4

You Are My Forever Love

One look at our culture can certainly bring discouragement. People embrace and reject one another even before marriage in a self-centered frenzy to find the one that makes them feel good about themselves. And hearts get broken. With all that going on, it is hard to remember what real love looks like.

Father, I have learned the shocking truth that no human on this earth can deliver the intimacy my heart desires so deeply. No person can love me with all the unconditional love I crave or give me the sense of security and identity I search so hard to find.

You give me a glimpse of a love that is true in Your book of Song of Solomon. A story of love from beginning to end, it takes me on the journey of a couple who has eyes for no other. Lord, I think of You and how You only have eyes for me. You long for me to understand unconditional love. Your love! Your truth tells me,

Place me like a seal over your heart, like a seal on your arm; for love is as strong as death, its jealousy

unyielding as the grave. It burns like blazing fire, like
a mighty flame (Song of Songs 8:6 NIV).

Only one love exists to satisfy those longings. You, Lord,
who made me, knows me, and pursues me, are the only one
who can fill that void. When I stop looking elsewhere and
receive the love You freely give, I finally find that ultimate
fulfillment. "It burns like blazing fire, like a mighty flame."
Fueled by You, the passion never burns out.

Lord, You have set Your gaze on me. No one and nothing
can come between me and Your declared love. My bond with
You can never be broken. I am Your forever love.

. . . .

As high as the heavens are above the earth,
so great is his love for those who fear him.
PSALM 103:11 NIV

You Are God Alone

Powerful God, You reminded me this morning that in the beginning, You spoke. When You did, the universe came into being. You formed the world and sustained life. I am in awe of You and Your wondrous creation. I love You, heavenly Father. Not only did You create and oversee the world, You so tenderly drew me into a relationship with You. Wonder of wonders! I'm Your child because You first loved me!

It breaks my heart that so many people miss this. They are living life and missing You. They are spiritually blind. They don't seek You. And they attribute Your magnificent, incomprehensible work to chance or meaningless gods.

What magnificent truth—You existed before our world ever began. There is no other God but You. Oh, the absolute delight to read what You said through Isaiah. Your truth tells me,

I am the LORD, and there is no other; Besides Me there is no God. I will gird you, though you have not known Me; that men may know from the rising to the setting of the sun that there is no one besides Me. I am the LORD, and there is no other, the One forming light and creating darkness, causing well-being and creating calamity; I am the Lord who does all these (Isaiah 45:5–7 nasb).

Lord, I will sing praises to You and Your wondrous creation. I love to share with others the truth that You are sovereign over all and that there is no other God but You. Thank You for loving me and calling me Your precious child.

. . . .

O Lord, there is none like You,
nor is there any God besides You, according to all
that we have heard with our ears.
1 Chronicles 17:20 nasb

You Are My Peace

Peace. Everyone longs for it—peace with others, peace within our families, peace in life, world peace. Jesus, You are my Prince of Peace. Your truth tells me,

> For to us a child is born, to us a son is given; and the government will be on his shoulders. And he will be called Wonderful Counselor, Mighty God, Everlasting Father, Prince of Peace (Isaiah 9:6 NIV).

But how do I handle my anxiety from the unexpected phone call in the middle of the night? Or the pain I see on my child's face when heartbreak strikes? Or the bill I receive that can't be paid?

You calm the storm inside me by whispering Your truth to my soul, "Peace I leave with you; my peace I give you. I do not give to you as the world gives. Do not let your hearts be troubled and do not be afraid" (John 14:27 NIV). You remind me that to experience Your peace I must believe You are who You say You are and will do what You say You will do. "I have told you these things, so that in me you may have peace. In this world you will have trouble. But take heart! I have overcome the world" (John 16:33 NIV). As long as my faith and focus are on You, I will have access to Your peace. I can weather any storm if I hold on to the hand who controls it. It's when I lose sight of You and concentrate on the whirling circumstances around me that I lose my peace and panic, instead.

You remind me that if my roots are anchored deep in Your truth, I am better equipped to not only withstand the flood of anxiety, but sail above it in Your perfect peace. I can simply turn to You, who can and will guard my heart and mind with Your peace that transcends all understanding. I cling to Your truth and promises in my life: "And the peace of God, which transcends all understanding, will guard your hearts and your minds in Christ Jesus" (Philippians 4:7 NIV). Lord, I trust in You. You are my Prince of peace.

· · · · · · · · · · · · · · · · · · · ·

Turn from evil and do good; seek peace and pursue it.
PSALM 34:14 NIV

You Are Truth

{ JEREMIAH }

I am often stirred by the words of others who talk about You—dynamic speakers and powerful authors. These people seem to experience a sense of heightened emotion or spiritual warmth that I don't always feel. I long for what they have and I come back for more, hanging on their every word. Lord, am I missing something here?

I hear Your Spirit in my heart asking if they are telling the truth. Is it possible that the message doesn't exactly match Your Word? There is only one way I know to find out— I must take what I hear and compare it to what Scripture says, and not just in isolated verses but in context. If it doesn't hold up to Your Word—no matter how pleasing or good the speaker or book in question might sound—it's not truth.

I am reminded of Jeremiah and how You called him to stand apart from the crowd. It was Your message for Your people that You hand-picked Jeremiah to preach. Your Word tells me to seek discernment:

> Do not listen to what the prophets are prophesying to you; they fill you with false hopes. They speak visions from their own minds, not from the mouth

of the Lord. . . . But which of them has stood in the council of the Lord to see or to hear his word? Who has listened and heard his word? (Jeremiah 23:16, 18 NIV).

Lord, I can't allow myself to believe something based on my feelings alone. I must root myself firmly in Your Scriptures and seek Your wisdom. You are perfect in all of Your ways, and I long to grow deeper in Your truth daily.

. . . .

You will seek me and find me
when you seek me with all your heart.
JEREMIAH 29:13 NIV

You Heal

{ LAMENTATIONS }

She cried out to You! Daughter Jerusalem had lost more than her houses, temple, and protective walls. She had lost the blessing from You who loved her most. Feeling like an orphaned child abandoned on the street to fend for herself, she cried out for help. Finally realizing the futility of her own efforts, she turned her heart toward home to see if anyone would hear.

Someone did. It was You, Lord, who promised never to abandoned Jerusalem. You listened to the lamentations of the prophet Jeremiah, accepted his openness and honesty, and led him to realize Your truth. Your prophet acknowledged the reality of Jerusalem's pain, saying her wound was as deep as the sea. And then he asked the question: who can heal her?

Only You, my Father. As Jeremiah walked through the stages of grief, naming his pain and questioning Your goodness, he came full circle. He remembered Your faithfulness, and it restored his hope. You would not punish forever. You would heal them and restore Your people.

When I walk through my next valley of sadness, I will remember Jeremiah's mournful song. I will pour my heart out fully, honestly, before You, who listens and cares. You will draw me close with everlasting comfort. Your truth tells me,

I well remember them, and my soul is downcast within me. Yet this I call to mind and therefore I have hope: Because of the LORD's great love we are not consumed, for his compassions never fail. They are new every morning; great is your faithfulness (Lamentations 3:20–23 NIV).

. . . .

Draw near to God and He will draw near to you.
Cleanse your hands, you sinners;
and purify your hearts, you double-minded.
JAMES 4:8 NASB

You Give Me a New Heart

{ EZEKIEL }

In You there is hope! In You there is life. No one on earth is too far gone, too separated from You to receive Your Spirit of life. I am in awe of Your powerful and amazing grace and Your relentless mercy, Lord. Just as You breathed hope into dry, brittle bones in the book of Ezekiel, You continue to breathe Your life into me and Your chosen people, restoring our souls and starting new life inside.

Your truth tells me in Ezekiel that You will give me a new heart if I continue to seek Your ways:

> I will give you a new heart, and a new spirit I will put within you. And I will remove the heart of stone from your flesh and give you a heart of flesh. And I will put my Spirit within you, and cause you to walk in my statutes and be careful to obey my rules (Ezekiel 36:26–27).

Gracious heavenly Father, Your presence in me is my joy, and I never want to know a single moment apart from You.

Protect my heart from the ways of the world because there are times that my soul feels as dry as those bones in the valley. But nothing is too hard for You who created me. You give me life, and You will not leave me!

Your Word reveals to me that, though Your people exchanged Your glory for passing pleasures and though they rebelled against You and defiled Your blessed land by engaging in detestable practices, You did not leave them. You cleansed them and restored them to the land in Your covenant faithfulness to them. You restored honor and glory to Your holy name throughout the nations, so that all would know that You are God alone. Yes, Lord, You are God alone! There is no other.

· · · · · · · · · · · · · · · · · · · ·

Blessed are those who keep his testimonies,
who seek him with their whole heart.
PSALM 119:2

You Are Honored

{ DANIEL }

Lord, for once I didn't cave to the approval of others. In that busy restaurant with the clinking glasses and jumbled conversations, I bowed my head and prayed. Even though I knew my long-lost friend might disapprove and the beautiful afternoon could come to an abrupt halt, I asked for Your blessing on the food anyway.

Lord, her surprised glare didn't intimidate me. My heart chose to honor You. I was inspired to stand firm through Your Word to Daniel—a man of integrity, full of obedience, who didn't compromise. He knew his God—He trusted You. And You granted him tremendous favor and knowledge. Others, instead of admiring him, listening to him, or emulating him, attempted to destroy him. He had been commanded to stop praying to You, yet he continued to bow in reverence to You. Your truth tells me,

> He went to his house where he had windows in his upper chamber open toward Jerusalem. He got down on his knees three times a day and prayed and gave thanks before his God, as he had done previously (Daniel 6:10).

O heavenly Father, if only the lost knew that Daniel's story points to a kingdom that is everlasting. If only the lost knew Daniel's story points to a greater example of courage and sacrifice: that Jesus stepped between sinners and Your judgment, giving eternal life to all who believe. If only the lost would seek Your amazing love.

In a world full of compromise, let my life shine in the light of Your glory. Daily I will bow my knee to You, and I will point the lost to Your amazing grace.

. . . .

Then I turned my face to the Lord God,
seeking him by prayer and pleas for mercy
with fasting and sackcloth and ashes.
DANIEL 9:3

You Set Me Apart

{ HOSEA }

I am not to love You in word only. I am to love You with all my heart. I ask You to turn my heart fully toward You so that Your Spirit will empower me to live out an obedient life worthy of my calling as Your beloved.

I wait for You like a bride who waits for her groom. And I pray that my heart remains pure. Your truth shows me how clear sin's devastation really is when I read about Hosea and the lives of the Israelites. Your heart, almighty God—the solution to their problems—seems so simple and clear. But heart rebellion leaves us all blind if we are not seeking You. As You explained in Hosea 5:4 (NIV): "Their deeds do not permit them to return to their God. A spirit of prostitution is in their heart; they do not acknowledge the LORD."

The Israelites' daily habits and routines didn't include You, God. You, pictured as the pure and faithful husband, burned with holy jealousy for Your bride. But over time, Your bride, the people, simply forgot You! Enthralled with the surrounding pagan cultures, their attention turned to the myriad false gods others served. Though they offered token sacrifices, the rest of their lives showed reliance on everything other than the One who could restore them. You. They didn't care to seek Your truth. And You called them out on their hypocrisy: "For I desire mercy, not sacrifice, and acknowledgment of God rather than burnt offerings" (Hosea 6:6 NIV).

The same is true today. Does my life reflect dependence on You, Lord—or on someone or something else? You do not want a holy facade. You want my heart. Your truth tells me,

> Love the Lord your God with all your heart and with all your soul and with all your mind (Matthew 22:37 NIV).

Lord, with all my heart . . . with all my soul . . . with all my mind, I do.

. . . .

Afterward the sons of Israel will return and seek the Lord
their God and David their king; and they will come trembling
to the Lord and to His goodness in the last days.
HOSEA 3:5 NASB

You Are My Stronghold

Lord, we need You now—*I* need you now! Without warning a raging storm hit, and life as I knew it will never be the same. It's hard to understand why You allow such devastation—natural disasters, mass shootings, and corruption—to touch our lives. Why?

I search for wisdom in the book of Joel. It says that one minute the field was there, ripe with grain ready for harvest. Then a swarm of locusts rolled in like a dark tsunami wave over the vegetation, consuming everything in its path. In an instant, the once lush and fertile field lay bare, stripped down to the naked earth, robbed of value, sustenance, and any sign of life.

Joel watched the phenomenon with his own eyes. Could he have imagined such immediate devastation otherwise? Yet You, God, had planned it as a warning for Your people. A warning that has echoed down to me. Judgment was coming! Israel had once stood as a beautiful lush field, flourishing under Your protective care, planted in a land You had given them. But they had grown wild. They had rejected Your personal touch and had turned to foreign gods instead. Though You had tilled and weeded and worked relentlessly to bring them back to a healthy relationship with You, they had insisted on spiritual starvation.

It's the same today. We have stripped You from our lives—our families, schools, and businesses. Your prophet Joel reminds me of Your sovereignty and goodness. Seemingly pointless tragedy becomes a tool in Your hands. The trials shape us—shape me—and keep my eyes focused on You, to seek Your wisdom and godliness as I surrender to Your lordship even in bad times. I know You are faithful to those who trust in You! It's not too late! Your truth tells me,

> The LORD will roar from Zion and thunder from Jerusalem; the earth and the heavens will tremble. But the LORD will be a refuge for his people, a stronghold for the people of Israel (Joel 3:16 NIV).

I will turn back to You!

. . . .

When the humble see it they will be glad;
you who seek God, let your hearts revive.
PSALM 69:32

You Rule over All

{ AMOS }

It's easy to see You in the good—to praise You in Your provision or Your healing. But what about when hard times come? When the provision doesn't appear or my loved one dies? Where are You then?

As I read the book of Amos, I am reminded that You, the God of the universe, are still in the same place You have always been—in control. Your truth tells me,

> He who forms the mountains, who creates the wind, and who reveals his thoughts to mankind, who turns dawn to darkness, and treads on the heights of the earth—the LORD God Almighty is his name (Amos 4:13 NIV).

There has never been a moment—and never will be—when You are not completely supreme over all that You have made. You are not only sovereign, You are just and You are completely good.

So what about the bad in life? While You are not the author of evil, You have the power and authority to work even the worst things in life for my good and for Your glory.

Thank You for being with me through those tough times. Sometimes the worst times are brought about by my own hand. You are sovereign, but You insist on holiness. In Israel's case, the catastrophes that came upon them were permitted by You as a means of loving discipline, to alert them to their sin. You were warning them of the consequences of their waywardness and imploring them to return to You.

It is in the difficulties of life that my faith is most refined. Will I trust in Your goodness and sovereignty, though everything I see with my eyes looks hopeless? Yes, Lord. I will walk by faith and cling to Your truth: "Now faith is confidence in what we hope for and assurance about what we do not see" (Hebrews 11:1 NIV). Lead me, Lord.

. . . .

Lead me in your truth and teach me, for you are the God of my salvation; for you I wait all the day long.
PSALM 25:5

You Humble Prideful Hearts

{ OBADIAH }

Why do I think I can oppose Your will and win? Have I tried to find life and meaning apart from Your plan? A quick glance into my own heart reveals the answer. O Lord, forgive my prideful heart. I know that whenever I live on my own resources instead of Yours, I discover the same sinister pride lurking in my heart that destroyed Edom.

You were not impressed with the Edomites, the descendants of Esau who lived in rocky fortresses southeast of Judah. From their very inception, their hearts had been bent on evil toward Your children. They persecuted the Israelites, delighted in their trials, worked toward their destruction. In their prideful hearts, they gloried in Judah's weakness and believed themselves to be invincible.

But You, God, are the ultimate defender. Even though Your words were few, Your humble servant Obadiah used them to deliver a powerful message on the lesson of worldly pride. Your truth tells me,

> "The pride of your heart has deceived you, you who
> live in the clefts of the rocks and make your home

on the heights, you who say to yourself, 'Who can bring me down to the ground?' Though you soar like the eagle and make your nest among the stars, from there I will bring you down," declares the LORD (Obadiah 3–4 NIV).

Only You—and anyone who belongs to You—will stand victorious in the end.

Lord, no matter how burdened I may seem now, I know that You are sovereign and will deliver me in Your time. You will take down every opposition to Your glory. I will trust in You alone to keep me in complete humility. Change my heart to keep it pure and in rhythm with Yours so that I can change the lives of others.

. . . .

The word of God is living and active, sharper than any two-edged sword, piercing to the division of soul and of spirit, of joints and of marrow, and discerning the thoughts and intentions of the heart.
HEBREWS 4:12

You Are Full of Compassion

{JONAH}

Lord, Your truth spoken to Jonah opened my eyes to Your unchangeable grace and mercy for others. You softened my heart against the enemies who attack my faith—those who worship other gods. You, sovereign God, knows the hearts of men; You are full of compassion and slow to anger.

I can understand how Jonah was furious at You for saving the people of Nineveh. In his mind they didn't deserve it, and he challenged Your ways. He wanted the Ninevites to pay for the evil they had done, especially to his own people. But You showed Your unfailing mercy, in the same way you show it to me. Your truth tells me,

"Should I not have concern for the great city of Nineveh, in which there are more than a hundred and twenty thousand people who cannot tell their right hand from their left?" (Jonah 4:11 NIV).

Knowing that we are all sinners bent on going our own way, You desire that we all be saved and come to the knowledge of Your truth. Oh, how Your words give me hope: "The wages of sin is death, but the gift of God is eternal life in Christ Jesus our Lord" (Romans 6:23 NIV). Through Christ's redemptive work on the cross, I am forgiven and given new life. A new life offered to all!

Lord, I choose mercy and forgiveness—even for my enemies. Guide me in Your way and not my own. Give me a heart that beats like Yours—a heart that is slow to anger and full of compassion. Empower me with Your strength and wisdom that I may share Your truth with those who are lost in this world and not seeking You.

. . . .

Teach me your way, O LORD, that I may walk in your truth;
unite my heart to fear your name.
PSALM 86:11

You Have Shown Me What Is Good

{ MICAH }

Why do I feel bound to control my situation? I read self-help books. I search the internet for solutions. I embrace the advice of professionals. But I still can't get it right. It's only when I seek Your wisdom, Your Word, that I find answers in my life. Everything I need is in Your Word. It's everything I need to be able to let go of control.

I praise Your holy name, Lord, as You show me in the book of Micah that duty had long before replaced delight and the Israelites were imprisoned in the hard shell of a religion that had left their souls withered and without hope. Some pressed on in spite of it all, while others abandoned their posts altogether, turning to foreign gods, which must have seemed easier.

What went wrong? In Your rich mercy and relentless love, You reasoned through the prophet Micah with their confused and wandering hearts—as You do with my heart. Micah does not deny the desirability of sacrifices. But did they really think more burnt offerings could be the solution? Did they think they could control Your purpose or manipulate Your thoughts?

Micah 6:8 sums up Your deepest desire to me. *"Enough with the show,"* You say, *"the empty offerings."* You want me to let go of the distractions of life and give You my heart. You want me engaged, so that I walk every day in true communion with You—the kind of intimacy that always brings repentance and molds my character into one that pleases You, that promotes justice, and is merciful and humble. Your truth tells me,

> He has shown you, O mortal, what is good. And what does the LORD require of you? To act justly and to love mercy and to walk humbly with your God (Micah 6:8 NIV).

You, Lord, my redeemer, promise never to leave me. I will walk humbly with You forever. Your truth for my life is the only thing I seek—for this is good!

. . . .

How can a young man keep his way pure?
By guarding it according to your word.
PSALM 119:9

You Are My Celebration

{ NAHUM }

You bring me comfort. You are my light in darkness. You are my compassionate King! I celebrate my life with joyful anticipation of all that You have in store for me. Some fear You and Your Word, but I find hope. I know that You are sovereign and You bring justice to the unjust!

You show me time and time again that You love Your children. Under Assyrian rule, Judah's hope had all but vanished, but Nahum's intense proclamation of Your judgment against their evil deeds rekindled their belief in Your goodness. Your people *would* again celebrate. They had hope knowing that Nineveh, their oppressor for generations, would soon come under Your judgment. You poured out Your justice and wrath at last on that evil city. You had promised it. It was as good as done! Your truth tells me,

> The LORD is slow to anger and great in power, and the LORD will by no means leave the guilty unpunished. In whirlwind and storm is His way, and clouds are the dust beneath His feet (Nahum 1:3 NASB).

Nahum's dark message of condemnation actually bears a powerful picture of hope for Your people—and for me. Even when surrounded by the seemingly worst possible situations, You see my pain, and Your compassion overflows. Your patience is perfect timing for the best revelation of Your glory.

Lord, use me to show others that You are to be celebrated. The measure of my joy—even in a difficult life—reveals the depth of my belief that You will prove faithful to Your promise. I have the prospect of eternal life in heaven with Jesus. Why let the worries of this world weigh down my soul? I know the day is coming when every tear will be erased, every broken relationship will be mended, and every person will know the pleasure of pure intimacy with You. Let the celebration begin!

. . . .

You, Lord, keep my lamp burning;
my God turns my darkness into light.
Psalm 18:28 niv

You Talk to Me

{ HABAKKUK }

Lord, You had a conversation with Habakkuk, and he wanted to know! As a prophet who shared Your heart and burden for Your people, he asked You for an explanation. He essentially prayed, "Lord, Your people pervert justice and promote violence. It's really awful down here. Why do You let their sin go unpunished?"

He wasn't prepared for Your answer: *Look among the nations! Observe! Be astonished! Wonder! Because I am doing something in your days You would not believe if you were told.* Then You unveiled Your plan to use evil Babylon to bring Your people to their knees. Under intense enemy oppression, Your people would finally break and return to You.

You helped him see that Your supremacy knows no bounds. You do not require Your people—including me—to understand Your will. You just ask us to obey it, even when it seems unreasonable. Help me obey!

You work through unbelieving hearts as well as Your own people's to accomplish Your will. Every circumstance in and under heaven bends to Your decree. I will trust You! Your truth tells me,

Yet I will exult in the LORD, I will rejoice in the God of my salvation (Habakkuk 3:18 NASB).

Your truth set Habakkuk free—it sets us all free! Judah's impending judgment would not be the end—only the means to Your ultimate end of reconciliation and joy. Through pain, Your people would see their need for the Savior You had already pledged to send. Though he knew captivity was bitter, Habakkuk could already taste the sweetness of Your salvation. And I have too!

O Lord, I love my conversations with You daily. My spirit hears Your voice as You graciously speak Your wisdom into my life. I may not always like or understand Your plans, but You are sovereign. That is enough for me.

. . . .

Let me hear what God the LORD will speak,
for he will speak peace to his people, to his saints;
but let them not turn back to folly.
PSALM 85:8

You Are My Mighty Warrior

L ord, thank You for warnings. Zephaniah warned Your people seven times! "The day of the Lord is near" (Zephaniah 1:7 NASB). Those words should make anyone stop in fear and seek Your truth. But the warning didn't stop the Israelites, and Your warnings don't always stop me.

Generation after generation, Your people have turned their backs on You—and many still do. They continued in their grievous sins, forsaking the only hope they ever had, You, Lord. But a remnant of Your people did understand. They knew You and feared You differently—a reverent fear for the Creator of the universe. I want to know You the way they did.

For those who didn't stray, You held out an incredible promise. You came not only to deliver them from their current circumstances but to give them an eternity of peace. Zephaniah describes You as a mighty warrior—strong, worthy, and brave. Breaking down Judah's prison's door, You rushed in and lifted her in Your powerful arms, then consoled her with joyful singing. I love the image of that. Her knight had finally come! Your truth tells me so beautifully,

The LORD your God is with you, the Mighty Warrior who saves. He will take great delight in you; in his love he will no longer rebuke you, but will rejoice over you with singing (Zephaniah 3:17 NIV).

This beautiful picture of You as our tender warrior provides a foundation for understanding what the apostle John later said about love: "There is no fear in love. But perfect love drives out fear, because fear has to do with punishment. The one who fears is not made perfect in love" (1 John 4:18 NIV). You are perfect! And when I know You are near, I feel safe. When I'm wrapped in Your powerful arms, my fears fade into joy.

Zephaniah reminds me that sin matters to You. It's why You sent Your Son to die. My hope lies in Jesus's provision. He makes my heart white as snow and prepares my soul for eternal life at His side. No more fear!

. . . .

Seek the LORD, all you humble of the earth who have carried out
His ordinances; seek righteousness, seek humility.
Perhaps you will be hidden in the day of the LORD's anger.
ZEPHANIAH 2:3 NASB

You Shake the Heavens and the Earth

{ HAGGAI }

It's been over 2,500 years since Haggai delivered his message from You to the Jews who had returned home from exile in Babylon. They had forgotten You and Your desolate temple, choosing instead to focus on their own interests, building and remodeling their own homes. To me, this a graphic illustration of Your people's misplaced priorities. But You encouraged Your people through Haggai, gently reminding them of their love for You and asking them to rebuild Your temple. If they put You first, then You would reveal Your future blessings and glory. It was a glimpse of Your precious Son, Jesus:

> "This is what the LORD Almighty says: 'In a little while I will once more shake the heavens and the earth, the sea and the dry land. I will shake all nations, and what is desired by all nations will come, and I will fill this house with glory,' says the LORD Almighty" (Haggai 2:6–7 NIV).

As I dig deeper into Your Word, almighty God, I find that You chose Zerubbabel, son of Shealtiel, governor of Judah, to lead Your people. You made him like Your signet ring, giving him honor and authority. Although he wasn't Your one and only Son, You established his part in the lineage that led to the One who was—Jesus. I am amazed how You unravel Your truth to me—that You no longer need an ornate temple of gold and precious stones. Your temple is Jesus. And because I am one with Him, Your Holy Spirit now dwells in me. O Father, You make me like Your signet ring too. Your truth tells me, "Do you not know that your bodies are temples of the Holy Spirit, who is in you, whom you have received from God? You are not your own; you were bought at a price" (1 Corinthians 6:19–20 NIV). Over 2,500 years ago, You thought of me.

. . . .

But may all who seek you rejoice and be glad in you;
may those who love your salvation
say continually, "Great is the LORD!"
PSALM 40:16

You Are the Lord of Hosts

{ ZECHARIAH }

From the very beginning, You, Lord of hosts, wanted to be with Your children. The problem was always their sin. It separated souls from each other, from You. But You would not give up. Thank You for never giving up. Thank You for putting Your plan in motion.

Though it looked like no hope lay on the horizon and Your children's sins were great, Your love was greater and You were sending Your Branch! Thank You for always sending help. Your truth tells me,

> Then say to him, "Thus says the LORD of hosts, 'Behold, a man whose name is Branch, for He will branch out from where He is; and He will build the temple of the LORD. Yes, it is He who will build the temple of the LORD, and He who will bear the honor and sit and rule on His throne. Thus, He will be a priest on His throne, and the counsel of peace will be between the two offices'" (Zechariah 6:12–13 NASB).

Through David's line, Zechariah said, You would send a Savior who would permanently end the power of sin over Your people. And You did! "I, Jesus, have sent My angel to testify to you these things for the churches. I am the root and the descendant of David, the bright morning star" (Revelation 22:16 NASB).

For those who believed Zechariah's message, it kindled enough hope to handle their current crisis. It also encouraged them to start afresh, living in the kind of selfless, proactively loving community You intended. It still kindles hope. With Your Spirit in our hearts, we can live with You in perfect righteousness, love, and community.

Lord, this is my hope. Jesus is alive, fulfilling every true prophet's predictions and bridging the gap that once separated me from You. Now heaven waits for all those who have placed their hope in You. Heaven waits for me! Let me branch out to others so that they will seek truth and Your great love.

. . . .

I will bring them back and they will live in the midst
of Jerusalem; and they shall be My people,
and I will be their God in truth and righteousness.
ZECHARIAH 8:8 NASB

You Remain the Same

{ MALACHI }

Lord, as I reminisce about my past, I realize I've come a long way. You, heavenly Father, guided me through it all. My choices and decisions must have caused You sorrow at times, but You never abandoned me.

I think about the Israelites. Lord, from the garden of Eden to the flood to the promise of Abraham, Your hand always guided their steps, just like You continue to do for me today. I think about Isaac, Jacob, Joseph, and Egypt, where Your people multiplied in number. Though generations came and went, You, who had called them from the beginning, stood faithful: faithful through their deliverance from Egypt, through forty years of complaining and unbelief in the desert, through victories in Canaan under the leadership of Joshua, the judges, and kings such as David. Faithful even as Your people fell apart, chasing other gods instead of You who loved them. Thank You for Your steadfast love and faithfulness!

Lord, I think about all the years of heartache, infidelity, idolatry, and oppression. You stayed near, and Your love never wavered. Malachi, Your last prophet of Israel, heard You speak truth: I have loved you (Malachi 1:2 NIV).

Then You were silent for four hundred years before Your plan unfolded. I can't imagine Your silence in my life, not even for one day.

Better than any earthly romance, You, the God of the universe, remained in love with the remnant of people still following You. You show me through Your Word that though Israel had changed, Your faithfulness remained, fueled by a passion that would span the next four hundred years when Your promise would culminate in the coming of Your Son, Jesus Christ—my Savior and Redeemer.

Though thousands of years have passed between Malachi's time and today, sin hasn't changed much. We still fall short of Your glory and desperately need Your guidance. And even though I, too, fall short, You have set me free from my sins and given me the gift of Your grace through Your Son, Jesus. Your promises are true!

. . . .

"I will send my messenger, who will prepare the way before me.
Then suddenly the Lord you are seeking will come to his temple;
the messenger of the covenant, whom you desire, will come,"
says the Lord Almighty.
MALACHI 3:1 NIV

You Take the Blame

I humbly fall at Your feet this morning. You know the depths of my heart and how my heart shatters when I hear the words, "It's your fault." I've heard this phrase many times throughout my life—and whether directed at me or at someone else, every time, I feel the heavy weight of blame. Why do I blame myself for the unhealthy choices that a family member or a friend has made in life? Why do I take the blame for their misfortunes?

The world shows me that nobody is immune to this behavior—great-grandparents, grandparents, parents, children, and grandchildren. They've all experienced it, and now it's my turn. It's the generational blame game. We blame the previous generation for the questionable choices we make in our lives. Lord, I place this problem in Your hands. Show me how to win this game by ending it once and for all.

You, the Lord of all the earth, have shown me through Your Word that it's an individual choice—that there will be conflicts between those who follow You and those who choose to follow the world. And there will be divisions in my own family and relationships if one person is living in the light and the other in the dark. Harmony is impossible, or so it seems to me. Your truth tells me,

Anyone who loves their father or mother more than me is not worthy of me; anyone who loves their son or daughter more than me is not worthy of me. Whoever does not take up their cross and follow me is not worthy of me. Whoever finds their life will lose it, and whoever loses their life for my sake will find it (Matthew 10:37–39 NIV).

King of heaven and earth, I pray this morning for those who have walked away from Your love. My heart cries over their separation—to be separated from You for eternity is an unbearable thought. Jesus, open their eyes to seek Your grace. Open their ears to hear Your truth and promise that they are Your children and You do not want them to perish. Lead them to Your cross. Only then will the blame game be over. "The Lord is not slow in keeping his promise, as some understand slowness. Instead he is patient with you, not wanting anyone to perish, but everyone to come to repentance" (2 Peter 3:9 NIV).

· · · · · · · · · · · · · · · · · · ·

The discerning heart seeks knowledge,
but the mouth of a fool feeds on folly.
PROVERBS 15:14 NIV

You Are My Light

I'm astonished, God, at how You reveal Your presence in even the most tense circumstances. A flight delay infuriated the young man sitting next to me. His anger burned as I quietly listened to him venting his current frustrations, which led to his unhappy past. I waited patiently for You to give me the specific words to share with him. And when You did, I was able to share how You had changed my life. Lord, as his face softened, he revealed to me that no one had ever shared Your love and peace with him. Jesus, how can that be?

We live in the information age, an era where thoughts and ideas move around the globe instantaneously. Today's technology allows human communication on a level unparalleled in human history. Yet even though we have these capabilities, Your children are not sharing the most important message of all—Your truth. It breaks my heart!

I, too, often fail to share Your love, grace, and peace with those who need You. Our families are in crisis. Fear bombards our children in their schools. Marriages fall apart. People are angry, and our world longs for You.

O Light of the World, I humbly fall to my knees to ask You that I may be Your light to those who cross my path. Let me never miss Your divine appointments. As I live in Your peace, I vow to live for Your glory. My life—in speech and action—will differ drastically from the world, but I pray that the difference will draw people's attention to You. The world is desperate for You. Reading the book of Matthew, I am reminded,

> Neither do people light a lamp and put it under a bowl. Instead they put it on its stand, and it gives light to everyone in the house. In the same way, let your light shine before others, that they may see your good deeds and glorify your Father in heaven (Matthew 5:15–16 NIV).

Lord, be my light.

. . . .

Your word is a lamp for my feet, a light on my path.
PSALM 119:105 NIV

You Open Doors

Today, Lord, I turned unknown visitors away. My heart pounded as I abruptly closed my front door. I knew who they were—people who claim to know You, but they misinterpret Your Word. As I stood behind the closed door, my heart rate increased. I knew my actions were wrong. I heard Your Spirit speak to my heart, *"Go after them and share the truth."* I opened my door and obeyed!

Holy Father, if only they could see the full, completed picture of Your infinite plan of salvation found only in Your Son, Jesus Christ. I think of Matthew and how he referred to the Old Testament at least 130 times, meticulously showing how the events of Christ's birth, ministry, death, and resurrection fulfilled each one of the prophecies made about my Savior from Scripture long ago.

Using Jesus's own words and miracles as further evidence, he demonstrated how Your kingdom, brought through Your Son, had a radically different look and purpose than the Jews had ever supposed. You had brought an even better deliverance, one that would extend to include anyone who "knocked" or sought refuge in Your Son. Best of all, Jesus would return to earth as the triumphant King and Savior of Your people, ready to judge and end evil while opening the door to eternal life with You. Your truth tells me,

> Everyone who asks receives, and the one who seeks finds, and to the one who knocks it will be opened (Matthew 7:8).

Your invitation to truth still remains, and many still haven't heard but they misconstrue Your Word. I'm in awe that Your Spirit indwells me and gives me Your words to speak boldly so that I can carry the gospel of Christ to the ends of the earth, starting outside my front door.

. . . .

"She will bear a son, and you shall call his name Jesus,
for he will save his people from their sins."
All this took place to fulfill what the Lord had spoken
by the prophet: "Behold, the virgin shall conceive
and bear a son, and they shall call his name Immanuel"
(which means, God with us).
MATTHEW 1:21–23

You Are My King Who Serves

{ MARK }

I love to learn from You! I think of what You must have felt—knowing that the weight of the world rested on Your shoulders, the weight of our sins. My sins! Even as You were overwhelmed by sorrow and knew that painful scourging, humiliating mocking, and excruciating crucifixion lay ahead, You didn't waver in Your purpose. You served! You took off Your outer garment and began washing Your disciples' feet, knowing Your time was near. What an incredible example of Your amazing love.

Sometimes, in my fatigue and weakness, I am tempted to feel sorry for myself. But if I want to be like You, Jesus, if I want my life to count for Your kingdom, I cannot live just for myself. You served all the way to Your death. You died for me! And if I am to be Your follower, I will take the focus off of my circumstances and wash the feet of others. Your truth tells me,

Sitting down, Jesus called the Twelve and said, "Anyone who wants to be first must be the very last, and the servant of all" (Mark 9:35 NIV).

He continued with His message: "Whoever wants to be first must be slave of all. For even the Son of Man did not come to be served, but to serve, and to give his life as a ransom for many" (Mark 10:44–45 NIV).

Jesus, my heart is a servant's heart—a heart that is ready to serve all whom You've called into my life. I seek Your eyes, Your ears, Your ways as I build up others in love and grace so that You will receive honor and glory.

. . . .

Glory in His holy name; let the heart of those who seek the LORD be glad.
PSALM 105:3 NASB

You Are the Talk of the Town

{ MARK }

Jesus, You were the talk of the town. How could You not be? Actually, everyone was aware of Your unusual teaching. Hordes of people hounded You, hoping to hear Your message and witness the miracles You performed everywhere You went. When You left the world, others carried on Your message, even to the point of persecution. Would I have been as brave?

I think of John Mark. He could have cowered in shame. Having abandoned his post out of fear, he was reprimanded and rejected from further partnership with Paul in his missionary journeys. How humiliating that must have been. But You didn't give up on him. You sent Barnabas to encourage him, just as You send people to encourage me. Barnabas showed grace and welcomed this young man—a believer since childhood—to a second chance at kingdom work alongside him and the apostle Peter.

Within a short time, John Mark grew to be a great leader in the early church, seeking You and flourishing under godly instruction. I want to grow like that—to flourish—and seek You more. Paul reconciled with John Mark later as he realized

Your power at work within him and saw his passion for pointing others to You.

Your Word tells me to seek Your truth daily and then I, too, will see Your power in my life:

He said to them, "Pay attention to what you hear: with the measure you use, it will be measured to you, and still more will be added to you. For to the one who has, more will be given, and from the one who has not, even what he has will be taken away" (Mark 4:24–25).

Oh, how I love to sit at Your feet and learn Your truth daily. I don't want to be the talk of the town, but I want to follow the One who was. Thank You for giving me countless second chances to be Your brave servant and share Your indescribable grace with those You bring into my life.

. . . .

Every word of God proves true;
he is a shield to those who take refuge in him.
PROVERBS 30:5

You Are Good

Jesus, You are calling me to learn Your Word. You open my eyes to what is true. When the rich man asked what he needed to do to get into heaven, You focused on the word *good*. What was Your point—and why didn't You answer the question directly?

Little did the man know that You, Jesus, had already gone straight to the heart of the matter. The rich man didn't need another method; he needed to know that You were the way to eternal life. You brought light to my question as You turned *his* question back around and revealed Your identity.

Lord, I understand! The Jews of Your day knew from the books of Psalms, Isaiah, and other Scriptures that only God the Father was holy. Everyone else was sinful. So You wanted the rich man and those listening to consider whether You were truly good. If You were (and no one could deny it), then You must be God. If You were God, then Your words were not merely good teaching. They were life giving, and You were life. Your truth tells me,

As Jesus started on his way, a man ran up to him and fell on his knees before him. "Good teacher," he asked, "what must I do to inherit eternal life?" "Why do you call me good?" Jesus answered. "No one is good—except God alone" (Mark 10:17–18 NIV).

Jesus, many people today want to take the rich man's approach. I did too, until I learned and studied Your words. They know You were a good man, but they stop short of seeking You or recognizing Your deity. They hope their record of good deeds will carry them to heaven, without ever realizing how even one small sin separates them infinitely from the Father's impeccable righteousness.

We must let go of our self-righteous efforts and cling to You, the only One who is good enough to cover our guilt by Your own perfection. You are good!

. . . .

It is easier for a camel to go through the eye of a needle than for someone who is rich to enter the kingdom of God.
MARK 10:25 NIV

You Are Jehovah-Rapha

{ LUKE }

I praise You in the stillness of the night as I sit humbly at Your feet. I wait patiently to hear Your loving voice, to feel the power of Your healing, for my body is weak and aches with pain. Oh, I seek the healing touch that comes only from You. All the way back in Deuteronomy, You made it clear that You are the God who heals. Your truth tells me, "I have wounded and I will heal, and no one can deliver out of my hand" (Deuteronomy 32:39 NIV).

I think about the woman reaching for You in the midst of the crowd and her determination to touch You. She was unclean and forbidden to worship in the temple. Anyone she touched would become unclean, including You, Jesus. Desperate for healing, she knew that by merely touching Your garment, she would be healed. Her faith was unshakable:

A woman who had a hemorrhage for twelve years, and could not be healed by anyone, came up behind Him and touched the fringe of His cloak, and immediately her hemorrhage stopped. And Jesus said, "Who is the one who touched Me?" And while they were all denying it, Peter said, "Master, the people are crowding and pressing in on You." But Jesus said, "Someone did touch Me, for I was aware that power had gone out of Me." When the woman saw that she had not escaped notice, she came trembling and fell down before Him, and declared in the presence of all the people the reason why she had touched Him, and how she had been immediately healed. And He said to her, "Daughter, your faith has made you well; go in peace" (Luke 8:43–48 NASB).

You calm my spirit, Jesus, as I reach out to touch the fringe of Your cloak, for You know my impurities and the need for healing. It's only touching You that changes my uncleanliness to complete healing. My faith is in You, Lord. You are Jehovah-Rapha—my God who heals.

. . . .

He sent out his word and healed them,
and delivered them from their destruction.
PSALM 107:20

You Saw Mary's Eyes

{ LUKE }

Lord, I just wanted everything to be perfect. Christmas dinner was a few hours away. You know how I am—my home had to be spotless. I felt I had to pull out my best dishes, prepare a fabulous meal, and try to keep it all together. There was so much to do, and not one person was helping me.

Then You, Jesus, stopped me. You interrupted my condemning attitude. You reminded me about Martha and how she noticed that her sister was sitting and listening to You speak, even though she still had several unchecked items on her to-do list. Just like me. Irritated with Mary's neglect to help, she appealed to You. Couldn't You see the injustice in the situation? I could. But Your truth tells me,

> Martha was distracted with all her preparations; and she came up to Him and said, "Lord, do You not care that my sister has left me to do all the serving alone? Then tell her to help me." But the Lord answered and said to her, "Martha, Martha, you are worried and bothered about so many things; but only one thing is necessary, for Mary has chosen the good part, which shall not be taken away from her" (Luke 10:40–42 NASB).

What You saw (that I often miss) was Mary's eyes seeking You and not the endless distractions that diverted Martha's attention. What one thing was really needed? You, Lord—not the matching plates or perfectly executed meal. You were the center attraction, the glory in the occasion. It was You! It still is You. You were the glorious occasion. Martha had forgotten, and You gently reminded her. And You gently remind me.

Lord Jesus, I love You. Thank You for encouraging me to calm the clamor of my life and sit daily at Your feet. When I seek Your way, then I will be able to keep it all together.

• • • • • • • • • • • • • • • • • •

O send out Your light and Your truth,
let them lead me; let them bring me
to Your holy hill and to Your dwelling places.
PSALM 43:3 NASB

You Stand in Front of Me

{ JOHN }

I squander so much precious time searching for things that I think will fulfill me—the perfect love, financial stability, acceptance from others—only to get my heart broken. Why am I influenced by the world's opinions regarding my happiness?

As I searched Your Word this morning, You opened my eyes to the fact that sometimes my tears blind me from seeing and trusting You, Jesus. I seek what the world states will bring happiness and contentment. I know it's a lie. Only You can satisfy my wants and desires. Only You!

You asked Mary the same question I hear You asking me when my eyes are blinded by tears:

When she had said this, she turned around and saw Jesus standing there, and did not know that it was Jesus. Jesus said to her, "Woman, why are you weeping? Whom are you seeking?" Supposing Him to be the gardener, she said to Him, "Sir, if you have carried Him away, tell me where you have laid Him, and I will take Him away" (John 20:14–15 NASB).

Jesus, You stand in front of me all the days of my life, and I let the tears of this world blind me. I know You will never forsake me because I belong to You. Your truth tells me:

> To all who did receive him, who believed in his name, he gave the right to become children of God (John 1:12).

I will commit my life to You. You are my perfect love. You are my rock. You accept me with open arms. Jesus— my eyes see clearly now.

. . . .

I love those who love me,
and those who seek me diligently find me.
PROVERBS 8:17

You Make Me Free

{ JOHN }

This morning I woke up early, around two. There wasn't a strange noise or a child crying. Jesus, it was You. You woke me up to make me think about what I'd done. My heart was aching because I'd chosen to make a decision without seeking Your wisdom first. I didn't pray, and the decision has caused me a lot of remorse. Now, in the early morning, I'm stuck without sleep, wondering how to move forward.

As I waited in prayer, I remembered what You said: "In the beginning was the Word, and the Word was with God, and the Word was God" (John 1:1 NASB). My heart heard You whisper, *"My child, continue in My Word and You will know the truth."*

I thought about You in the desert for forty days when You were tempted by the devil. You were tired. You were vulnerable, and this was the perfect time to be tempted. I am not sure I could have withstood the very first temptation. The devil offered You a shortcut to the dominion of the world by worshipping him instead of our heavenly Father. Could I have refused? He knew that if You accepted his offer, then Your purpose of dying on the cross would mean nothing, and I would be lost and dead in my sins. Eternal life with You would not exist. But You kept Your eyes on Your Father. You chose His perfect plan, which included me and the rest of Your children. Your truth tells me,

> "I give them eternal life, and they will never perish, and no one will snatch them out of my hand. My Father, who has given them to me, is greater than all, and no one is able to snatch them out of the Father's hand. I and the Father are one" (John 10:28–30).

My sweet Savior, I am captivated by Your love. You never leave me in the desert. You never leave me in my early hours. You are near. You show me the way. I am forgiven.

. . . .

So Jesus was saying to those Jews who had believed Him,
"If you continue in My word, then you are truly disciples
of Mine; and you will know the truth,
and the truth will make you free."
JOHN 8:31–32 NASB

You Are My Shepherd

So many people want to widen the gate. They may accept You, Jesus, as a good man, but they also welcome other deities, or they say that we all have the same God but we worship differently. They try to get closer to You, claiming all efforts to reach You are equally worthy. O Jesus, they live in an atmosphere of deception! You are the one true God and the only way to salvation. And the way to You is through a narrow gate.

You wanted the people to understand Your teaching, so You spoke in concrete pictures we could comprehend. Using the familiar metaphor of shepherd and sheep, You first described Yourself as the gate through which Your sheep came and went. You said that anyone who tries to enter the pen another way is a thief, intent on stealing or destroying Your sheep.

You are the good Shepherd who cares for the sheep. You know which of us are Yours, and we know You. We follow only Your voice because all others lead to danger and death. Only with the Shepherd can we find safety through the gate of salvation. Your truth tells me,

I am the gate; whoever enters through me will be saved. They will come in and go out, and find pasture. The thief comes only to steal and kill and destroy; I have come that they may have life, and have it to the full (John 10:9–10 NIV).

Oh, how I love my Shepherd. I know Your voice, and You know mine. I will follow You all the days of my life. There is only one way to You. I enter Your grace through the gate of my Savior. It is Your gate alone. It is in Your pasture that I find abundant and eternal life.

. . . .

My sheep hear my voice, and I know them,
and they follow me.
JOHN 10:27

I Am the Way, Truth, and Life

{ JOHN }

You've taken me to an unknown territory—an isolated place where the ocean waves crash against the seashore, warning me that a storm is near. It is here in my exile that You open my eyes to the truth that You alone are God. It is here, heavenly Father, that You pull me close to You through Your Word, Your truth, and ask me, *"Whom are you seeking?"*

Lord, it is You. I seek You and Your truth for my life! It breaks my heart that I have wasted precious time seeking after distractions that have diverted my attention away from Your love and grace.

Heavenly Father, You have revealed to me that You want me to know You more deeply—to love Your Word, to trust You, to seek You, and to know there is no other way to have eternal life with You except through Your Son, Jesus. Your truth tells me,

> Jesus said to him, "I am the way, and the truth, and the life. No one comes to the Father except through me" (John 14:6).

Father, there is no other way. You gave Your one and only Son so that through His death, I would have eternal life with You. Through His sacrifice, the veil was torn that separated me from You so that I could enter into Your throne room, the Holy of Holies. It's only through Jesus that I can stand before You without fear and trembling because He stands in front of me. You see me through Your precious Son, who knew no sin. Through Him I am pure, I am righteous, I am holy, and I am white as snow.

Now as my quiet time ends, You reveal to me that this is my beginning—to know You more deeply, to love Your Word, and to trust You all the days of my life. You are God alone. You are truth. Heavenly Father, it is You whom I seek; I seek truth.

. . . .

For God so loved the world, that he gave his only Son,
that whoever believes in him should not perish
but have eternal life. For God did not send his Son
into the world to condemn the world, but in order
that the world might be saved through him.

JOHN 3:16–17

You Reign

{ ACTS }

I can only imagine what the disciples were witnessing! As You slowly rose off the ground and ascended into heaven, I'm sure their gaze followed. Standing below, Your followers must have been filled with a strange, new hope. This was not the end, they realized. Your kingdom, Jesus, had only begun.

And then You sent Your Holy Spirit to fill Your people, just as You had promised. You told them a Helper was coming. And suddenly, the same men whose faith had wavered under simpler circumstances now surged with conviction and power as they preached even through persecution. You are the Son of God! And they devoted their lives to proclaiming faith in You as the key to salvation. To have been there . . . to have seen it with my own eyes! It is so hard to grasp.

Your truth tells me,

> There is salvation in no one else; for there is no other name under heaven that has been given among men by which we must be saved (Acts 4:12 NASB).

Lord, I love to meditate on Your words in the book of Acts. You give me a clear and glorious glimpse into what You intend for me and Your followers. No one was left out of the call. You equipped each believer to carry out the Great Commission, and You sent Your Holy Spirit to live inside of us—inside me—to guide us through life! And to me and to all the believers, the matter is clear: We have life-giving power for a lost and dying world. No power of darkness can stop Your sovereign hand.

Your power is alive today! You, Lord, who are the same yesterday, today, and forever, still work through Your people. You work through me! But sadly, so many people don't understand. They don't seek You. They resort to programs over relationships, strategies instead of Your Spirit. If only they would center their lives on Your Scripture and return to You, they would see that You are the risen King who reigns on Your throne. May Your kingdom come and Your will be done on earth as it is in heaven.

. . . .

It shall come to pass that everyone who calls upon the name of the Lord shall be saved.
Acts 2:21

You Will Not Be Silenced

{ ACTS }

Jesus, it breaks my heart when I think about our kids to-day attending public events. I remember the days when we were allowed to pray in schools or before sports games. We were encouraged to follow the Ten Commandments. And we were allowed to talk about our faith.

But times have changed. We have been silenced. What happened? Why have the laws limited Your followers' free-dom in the name of religious tolerance? What are we to do?

You speak to my heart as I read in Acts that Your dis-ciples could relate. Preaching the gospel in their day wasn't any easier. For them, telling others about You meant risking their very lives. Yet driven by their love for You and the firm belief that You would use their obedience for Your glory, they gladly opened their mouths and offered up their lives. Your truth tells me,

> "We gave you strict orders not to teach in this name," he said. "Yet you have filled Jerusalem with your teaching and are determined to make us guilty of this man's blood." Peter and the other apostles

replied: "We must obey God rather than human beings!" (Acts 5:28–29 NIV).

Though the persecution I may face pales in comparison to that which other people suffer (I think about Your missionaries in foreign lands), I still cringe under the judgment of those who ridicule my belief in You. It's so tempting to take the easier road, staying silent about my faith. Lord Jesus, please forgive me! Before I skip out on the next opportunity to speak about You, I will remember Peter's admonition to those who opposed the first believers: "We must obey God rather than human beings!" I will not be silenced.

. . . .

I said, "Who are you, Lord?" And the Lord said,
"I am Jesus whom you are persecuting."
ACTS 26:15

You Redeem Me

{ ROMANS }

Will You really forgive me? Shamed by my guilt, I often assume that no respectable human being—let alone You, God Almighty—would want anything to do with me. I know others have the opposite feeling: puffing themselves for being "good people," perhaps even devoutly religious, they assume You have no reason to condemn them, even though they may do little to nurture a personal relationship with You.

Lord, I see in the book of Romans that people in Paul's day may have had similar attitudes. Some may have felt trapped in their inability to please You, the God of the universe. Others prided themselves in their spiritual assets—particularly in comparison to the hopelessly lost Gentiles. Paul shattered both lines of mistaken thinking and reiterated how hopelessly depraved we all are, reminding us that we are headed for destruction unless we turn back to You. In his first letter to Timothy, Paul went so far as to claim that he himself was "the worst of sinners" (1 Timothy 1:16).

But You, heavenly Father, give us hope! You give me hope that my sins pave the way for a greater revelation of Your glory. Your truth tells me,

For all have sinned and fall short of the glory of God, and all are justified freely by his grace through the redemption that came by Christ Jesus (Romans 3:23–24 NIV).

When I realize my sin doesn't stifle Your goodness or Your grace but instead magnifies it through Your Son's all-sufficient sacrifice, I can stop shrinking back into my despair. You, my gracious and forgiving God, have redeemed me through Your one and only Son. I am lifted up out of my shame by Your loving hand.

. . . .

There is no one righteous, not even one; there is no one
who understands; there is no one who seeks God.
All have turned away, they have together become worthless;
there is no one who does good, not even one.
ROMANS 3:10–12 NIV

You Are My Rock

While You, Jesus, were on earth, the masses followed You everywhere. You were kind, compassionate, and bent on serving others. Just like You are today. You spoke with authority, yet with kindness, unlike any other. You brought hope and healing to the hurting around You. So why would Paul, one of Your most devoted followers, call You a stumbling stone? How could You, who are perfect, pose such a problem to some people?

When You promised through the prophets to send a Savior to rescue His people from sin, You were there. In Your perfect time, You were sent to live, die, and rise again as the payment for our sins—my sins. However, as I read Paul's letter, I'm reminded that the gift of salvation had to be accepted back then, the same as it does today. And that means surrendering our lives—my life—in exchange for the abundant life and eternal forgiveness that are offered to everyone who puts their faith in You.

Jesus, I understand now. That's exactly where people stumble. Your truth tells me,

They stumbled over the stumbling stone. As it is written: "See, I lay in Zion a stone that causes people to stumble and a rock that makes them fall, and the one who believes in him will never be put to shame" (Romans 9:32–33 NIV).

Everyone is happy to believe that You love them and have a plan for their life. Many even like the challenge of living morally clean lives. But to admit that they are hopeless sinners, utterly dependent on You alone to be saved? That's the death of pride and self that many refuse to accept.

Jesus, I embrace You. Your provision of forgiveness is the rock of life that brings me back to You.

. . . .

For who is God besides the LORD?
And who is the Rock except our God?
PSALM 18:31 NIV

You Bring Us Together

{ ROMANS }

Over two billion people live on this planet. Lord, You created us all different! Sometimes it seems as though it would have been easier if we didn't have differing opinions or ideas or conflicting backgrounds and personalities. But You chose to bring us together in a different way—through You, Jesus.

In his letter to the Romans, Paul unpacked Your amazing gospel message. At the end, he drove the point of it all home: glorify You, God, with one mind and voice. Your truth tells me,

> May the God who gives endurance and encouragement give you the same attitude of mind toward each other that Christ Jesus had, so that with one mind and one voice you may glorify the God and Father of our Lord Jesus Christ (Romans 15:5–6 NIV).

Lord Jesus, my faith grows daily as I hear Your voice through the Bible. I am grateful that I can have the attitude of mind that You have. I listen to Your heart, spoken through Your Word. I see, through the gospel accounts, how You lived and listened to Your Spirit, who helps me comprehend Your wisdom and truth.

As I lean hard into You and Your example, my faith becomes unshakable. I long to love others with a nonjudgmental attitude and see them through Your eyes. Paul declares that our unity in You bonds Your followers together in the same forgiveness and grace. Color, gender, age, and socioeconomic status only add beauty and diversity at the foot of Your cross. Filled with Your Spirit and recognizing Your beauty in one another, we are free to speak in unity Your language of love and redemption to others. Through our unity with one another, the world will see You and Your glorious love.

Nothing is more beautiful than intimate fellowship with You, particularly as I worship together with my family— my brothers and sisters in Christ. Your children.

· · · · · · · · · · · · · · · · · · ·

So faith comes from hearing,
and hearing through the word of Christ.
Romans 10:17

You Want Me to Know

{ 1 CORINTHIANS }

Step into any bookstore and it becomes obvious: People have a lot of thoughts about many topics. Row after row, countless books exist to broaden my horizons, increase my knowledge, and allegedly make me a better person in the process. The options, in the Christian section alone, can seem overwhelming. But then I think of You.

Many Christians feel unqualified to tell others about You because of their lack of knowledge. Lord, if they would only take the time to seek Your Word and Your truth, they would be saved and their lives would change forever—eternally!

I reflect on the situation of Paul, Your servant—an accomplished student of Jewish law and a convert to Christianity. You called and equipped him to lead the churches in truth. Was he overwhelmed when he wrote 1 Corinthians to subdue the prideful, right the wrong teaching, and reunite a church that sin had divided? If he was, he trusted You. His insight into Your call to love and serve simplified the difficulties, and his writings point Christians even today to the truth we must walk in if we want to please You.

I feel like he wrote this letter to me. Through it I learned more about Paul's determination to know You better:

When I came to you, I did not come with eloquence
or human wisdom as I proclaimed to you the testimo-
ny about God. For I resolved to know nothing while
I was with you except Jesus Christ and him crucified
(1 Corinthians 2:1–2 NIV).

O Lord, I want to know You better! Jesus, I believe that
You paid for my sins by Your death on the cross and I am now
one with You. The same power that raised You from the dead
now works in me. I don't have to be theologically trained, in-
tellectually elite, or a well-versed follower to accomplish great
things for Your glory. You empower me to do all that You have
called me to do.

· · · · · · · · · · · · · · · · · · · ·

The word of the cross is folly to those who are perishing,
but to us who are being saved it is the power of God.
1 CORINTHIANS 1:18

You Provide Strength

{ 2 CORINTHIANS }

Why do I feel most confident when life is going the way it should—my way? I think about the other times—when feelings of failure and inadequacy creep in and rob me of joy. What exactly has changed in these opposing scenarios?

Lord, change my attitude when I equate success with happiness. When others esteem me, when I have no financial worries, and when I can check off all the items on my legalistic to-do list, I feel pretty good about myself. My problem occurs when life ties me to a list of rules or doesn't accommodate my ideals—when others disrespect me or I fail to live up to my own standards. The bad news is that whether I seem to be succeeding or failing, I am still helpless and hopeless. Apart from You, I can accomplish nothing of true worth.

But the good news is that You don't leave me there. Your truth tells me,

But he said to me, "My grace is sufficient for you, for my power is made perfect in weakness." Therefore I will boast all the more gladly about my weaknesses, so that Christ's power may rest on me. That is why, for Christ's sake, I delight in weaknesses, in insults, in hardships, in persecutions, in difficulties. For when I am weak, then I am strong" (2 Corinthians 12:9–10 NIV).

Oh, how I love that You provide grace and strength to all who come to You and accept these gifts. The key to Your strength is realizing that I have none of it on my own. It requires complete humility and dependence on You. But when I do let go of my own efforts or legalistic views and rest in You alone, my faith can't be shaken. It's rooted in who You are, my almighty God, who sustains me.

· · · · · · · · · · · · · · · · · · ·

The law was given through Moses;
grace and truth came through Jesus Christ.
JOHN 1:17 NIV

You Call Me Beloved

{ GALATIANS }

Just one touch of Your grace washes all my sins away. O Abba, Father, it doesn't matter what I have done or where I have been—You call me Your beloved, even when there is nothing lovely about me. I humbly fall on my knees in awe of Your incredible love for me.

All of my sins—past, present, and future—are forgiven through Your precious Son's blood. You gave Your one and only Son to die so that I could be called Your child and live forever with You! This is amazing grace, indeed:

> When the set time had fully come, God sent his Son, born of a woman, born under the law, to redeem those under the law, that we might receive adoption to sonship. Because you are his sons, God sent the Spirit of his Son into our hearts, the Spirit who calls out, "*Abba*, Father." So you are no longer a slave, but God's child; and since you are his child, God has made you also an heir (Galatians 4:4–7 NIV).

My loving Father, You didn't free me to continue to serve my sinful nature. Rather, You freed me from my bondage of sin to serve You—to seek and follow Your precepts for life. My time with You is not limited to Sundays. My life belongs to You—to share Your message of salvation with those You lead into my path. Your truth tells me,

I have been crucified with Christ; and it is no longer I who live, but Christ lives in me; and the life which I now live in the flesh I live by faith in the Son of God, who loved me and gave Himself up for me (Galatians 2:20 NASB).

You invite me to deeper intimacy through seeking Your truth—through your Word and Your Spirit. Sovereign God, You call me beloved. I am truly Yours, and You are truly mine. My prayer is that I continue to learn your Word and share with others that they, too, are called Your beloved. And You are my Abba, Father!

. . . .

Your word I have treasured in my heart,
that I may not sin against You.
PSALM 119:11 NASB

You Reveal the Mystery of Your Will

{ EPHESIANS }

Why would they look to an idol instead of You, the Lord of all creation? The goddess Artemis stretched tall and immense at the heart of Ephesus, surrounded by a temple so impressive it lured the hearts of those You loved to embrace the beauty and worship her stone-cold statue. With a culture so centered on idol worship, what chance did Your apostle Paul possibly have to penetrate Satan's stronghold?

With man, it was impossible. But with You, God, Paul had all the power in the universe on his side. In his missionary journeys, Paul shared that You, the living God, actually hear and care about us, unlike Artemis. You cared about the people of Ephesus, and you care about me! You cared about me before I was even born.

Yes, Lord, You knew all the days of my life before even one of them came to be (Psalm 139:16). Now in Ephesians, Paul explains how You in Your sovereignty and wisdom planned heaven and earth for one magnificent purpose: to reveal Your glory through Your Son, Jesus Christ:

He chose us in him before the foundation of the world, that we should be holy and blameless before him. In love he predestined us for adoption to himself as sons through Jesus Christ, according to the purpose of his will, to the praise of his glorious grace, with which he has blessed us in the Beloved. In him we have redemption through his blood, the forgiveness of our trespasses, according to the riches of his grace, which he lavished upon us, in all wisdom and insight making known to us the mystery of his will, according to his purpose, which he set forth in Christ as a plan for the fullness of time, to unite all things in him, things in heaven and things on earth (Ephesians 1:4–10).

With the mystery of Your will unveiled, why would anyone seek anything else?

. . . .

Stand therefore, having fastened on the belt of truth,
and having put on the breastplate of righteousness.
Ephesians 6:14

You Calm the Storm

The ocean waves crashed against the shore this morning as I searched for the perfect white shell—my prayer shell. I couldn't find it. But then I heard Your Holy Spirit speak to my heart, *"My precious child, search for a broken one and pray with joy for those who are broken, that I will calm their storm. I will calm your storm."*

It's easy for me to get discouraged over my own trials or the storms that others face, especially the ones that don't seem to go away. In those moments of frustration and brokenness, I draw near to You and I remember Your servant Paul and his perspective. He trusted You in all the circumstances of his life and continued to pray with joy, knowing You never abandon Your people. You will never abandon me! Through repentance, thanksgiving, and joyful prayer, I will see, in Your good timing, Your hand at work in my life and the lives of Your children. The storms will cease because of Your saving grace. You've promised me this, and Your truth tells me,

I am confident of this very thing, that He who began a good work in you will perfect it until the day of Christ Jesus (Philippians 1:6 NASB).

Heavenly Father, I cling to Your promise that it is Your good work that saves me from the storms of life. I long to do Your Will and draw near to You in everything I do.

. . . .

The LORD also will be a stronghold for the oppressed,
a stronghold in times of trouble; and those who know
Your name will put their trust in You, for You, O LORD,
have not forsaken those who seek You.

PSALM 9:9–10 NASB

You Are My Everything

{ COLOSSIANS }

I can't imagine my life without You. There isn't a moment that I am not on Your mind. You know everything about me—every little detail! And now I desire to seek everything about You.

I quietly listen to Your voice through Your Word. Lord, You show me through Paul's letter to the Colossians that when I commit my life to You, You enfold me in a beautiful, loving relationship with You. I become one with Your Spirit *right now* as You rule from Your heavenly throne:

> If then you have been raised with Christ, seek the things that are above, where Christ is, seated at the right hand of God. Set your minds on things that are above, not on things that are on earth. For you have died, and your life is hidden with Christ in God. When Christ who is your life appears, then you also will appear with him in glory (Colossians 3:1–4).

O Lord, Your love never fails me. It never ends. You satisfy my soul, and I am in awe that though my physical body is still tied to this earth, my spirit is free to commune with You in the heavenly realms, drawing all the strength and power I need to work out Your will. Your truth tells me,

> Whatever you do, whether in word or deed, do it all in the name of the Lord Jesus, giving thanks to God the Father through him (Colossians 3:17 NIV).

Keeping You in my sight at all times, my eyes see what You see. My heart aches for the lost who don't seek You and Your truth for their lives. Lord, I pray that I won't waste what little time I have here on pursuits that won't count for eternity but that I'll move forward with purpose and power, and increase Your heavenly treasure—the lives of others. Whatever I do, I will do it for You.

. . . .

If then you have been raised with Christ,
seek the things that are above, where Christ is,
seated at the right hand of God.
COLOSSIANS 3:1

You Change My Heart

{ 1 THESSALONIANS }

I am guilty! I often get caught up in my feelings. I understand how a stirring or convicting sermon or a touching song could cause people to flock to the front where they give and receive prayers for a new life. But then I wonder, Lord, if the conversion experiences are real. Did true surrender occur, or was it merely an outlet for a temporary emotion that will fade over time?

You alone know our hearts. You alone know mine. And You are deeply interested in all of them. No matter how outwardly convincing repentance may seem, You know whether or not Your Spirit has enabled others to truly turn their lives over to You. It is not for me to judge others. Paul says in 1 Thessalonians that there is one way to identify real, God-driven conversion: It happens with power, Your Holy Spirit, and deep conviction. When You are at work, *real* change happens in the heart. Heart change shows up in our attitudes and actions as Your Spirit empowers us to overcome sin patterns and live in the fullness of grace. Your truth tells me,

> For we know, brothers loved by God, that he has chosen you, because our gospel came to you not only

in word, but also in power and in the Holy Spirit and with full conviction. You know what kind of men we proved to be among you for your sake. And you became imitators of us and of the Lord, for you received the word in much affliction, with the joy of the Holy Spirit (1 Thessalonians 1:4–6).

Lord, as I embrace our hungry world with the gospel, eager to lead others to You, I will faithfully proclaim Your truth. You alone know my heart. And my heart belongs to You.

. . . .

For this reason we also constantly thank God that
when you received the word of God which you heard
from us, you accepted it not as the word of men,
but for what it really is, the word of God,
which also performs its work in you who believe.
1 Thessalonians 2:13 nasb

You Are Just

Life is not fair. It's hard for me to sit back and take the blows from someone who has purposefully hurt me. It's even harder when the attacker is a fellow believer. Lord, my first reaction is to strike back. But You stop me. Thank You for stopping me.

You show me that the Thessalonian believers didn't have it easy either. They were experiencing significant persecution—much more than I will ever experience. Their refusal to participate in normal social and cultic activities as they turned to You would have left non-Christian family members, friends, and associates feeling offended. So serving You resulted in conflict and isolation. How scary and lonely.

Under such circumstances, it's easy to see why the believers might have felt like fighting back or giving up. But Paul told them to steer clear of either tendency. Instead, he told them to keep their eyes on You. To seek Your truth!

Why? Because You are just. You will by no means clear the guilty. Your truth tells me,

God is just: He will pay back trouble to those who trouble you and give relief to you who are troubled, and to us as well. This will happen when the Lord Jesus is revealed from heaven in blazing fire with his powerful angels (2 Thessalonians 1:6–7 NIV).

Though it may look like evil has the upper hand, You promise to eventually take vengeance on those who have wronged Your people. You will vindicate Your children at the right time. I don't have to fight for my own cause because I have You, a Father who is far more righteous and qualified to render due judgment and punishment.

Because of who You are, I don't fight back and I don't give up. I persevere in the truth, knowing that when Jesus returns, I'll reap an eternal reward. In the meantime, I live and love with utter abandon, knowing that You, my Father, who sees and knows all that I endure, will make it right in the end.

. . . .

The wrath of God is revealed from heaven against
all ungodliness and unrighteousness of men,
who by their unrighteousness suppress the truth.
ROMANS 1:18

You Tell Me to Stand Firm

Does it really matter if I work for the Lord? I already know where I stand and where I'm headed. Lord, search my heart if I ever think those thoughts or become complacent or lazy in sharing Your truth with others.

Every morning when I rise, I think about You. I wonder what You will bring into my day and who I will touch with Your message of love and forgiveness. I think about Paul's first letter about Your imminent return and how some of the Thessalonians decided to pack up shop. *If Jesus is coming soon, why bother working anymore?* I'm puzzled by their thought process because they weren't thinking of others. Their lack of understanding hurt the believers who were tracking with the truth.

Lord, You are coming soon. Paul confirmed it, and I believe it. But much work needs to be done until that time, he explained. And it still does. Jesus, thank You for sharing with him detailed accounts of specific signs that You would send before the end of the world would come.

Protect me from the man of lawlessness, the one who will oppose and exalt himself against You, who is to come first.

Open the hearts of the unbelievers to Your truth, and expose his dark power and deception so they will not follow his lead.

When You return, Your arrival will leave no doubt. I long for that day when I see You accompanied by fire and mighty angels, and You swiftly end the evil one's reign with the simple power of Your breath. Then all Your people will unite—both those who are still living and those who have died—in eternal perfection and glory.

Your Word tells me through Paul to stand firm:

> So then, brothers, stand firm and hold to the traditions that you were taught by us, either by our spoken word or by our letter (2 Thessalonians 2:15).

Knowledge of Your return should not promote moral lethargy. Instead, it should propel us—propel me—to action, inviting all who will come to seek shelter in You, Lord Jesus, knowing that my work done in You is not in vain.

. . . .

We have become partakers of Christ, if we hold fast
the beginning of our assurance firm until the end.
HEBREWS 3:14 NASB

You Guide Me through Others

{ 1 TIMOTHY }

I often wonder if I did my best as a parent in teaching my children about You. What if they stumble in Your truth as they walk into adulthood?

You calm my soul as I read 1 Timothy. He knew Your Word. He knew You. He had learned about Your sacrificial love from the time he was a young boy. His mother and grandmother raised him in the knowledge of You, strengthening his heart even as he became a young man. I wonder if they felt the same way I do now as they let him go into the world.

Lord, my spirit tells me that Your timing is perfect. Timothy's mother and grandmother knew it was time to let You take all that they had poured into his young life and use it for Your kingdom. As they let him go, You brought Your chosen apostle Paul to take Timothy under his wing as his son in the faith, on a journey to share Your amazing grace and forgiveness. You didn't leave Your child, Timothy, on his own. Now it's my turn to see You take all that I poured into my children and trust You to bring others into their lives to further Your kingdom.

It encourages me how Paul mentored Timothy to continue walking in faith. Through his letter, Your truth tells me,

As for you, O man of God, flee these things. Pursue righteousness, godliness, faith, love, steadfastness, gentleness. Fight the good fight of the faith. Take hold of the eternal life to which you were called and about which you made the good confession in the presence of many witnesses (1 Timothy 6:11–12).

Lord, thank You for the godly friends You give us to encourage each other to reach the world.

. . . .

*If I am delayed, you will know how people ought
to conduct themselves in God's household, which is the church
of the living God, the pillar and foundation of the truth.*
1 Timothy 3:15 niv

You Train Me in Righteousness

{ 2 TIMOTHY }

These days I hardly need to leave my home. Shopping, social networks, education, medical advice, and an endless supply of resources are at my fingertips, just a click away. The only challenge is to sift through all the options to find what seems to be most reliable. What am I missing, Lord? Why can't I find the answers to my problems?

Your Spirit inside my heart tells me to restart my search with You! It pains me that I'm neglecting what You have taught me throughout the years—to go to the one place I can go to know and possess everything I need in life. Your Word! The Bible is more than just a guidebook, though it *is* that—it's Your guidebook for my life. It is more than a historical documentary or a poetic analogy, though it contains those elements too. Paul told us that Scripture comes from Your very breath. Just as Your breath raised Adam's lifeless form into a living creature, You have spoken Your words of life, recorded them through Your created beings, and revealed their truth and power through Your Holy Spirit. Your truth tells me,

All Scripture is breathed out by God and profitable for teaching, for reproof, for correction, and for training in righteousness, that the man of God may be complete, equipped for every good work. (2 Timothy 3:16–17).

As I open Your Scriptures and grasp Your Word in my hands, Your Spirit tells my heart to shut out the endless other resources at my fingertips. Only You can open my eyes to Your truth's incredible significance in every situation that I face.

. . . .

Do your best to present yourself to God as one approved,
a worker who has no need to be ashamed,
rightly handling the word of truth.
2 Timothy 2:15

You Are My Tower of Refuge

{ 2 TIMOTHY }

Betrayal. How can we ever get over the purposeful betrayal of our trust by others? Lord, as I walk the steps of Your path, You, my Shepherd, remind me that I can choose my direction. I can either follow You and forgive or remain in my bitterness.

O Wonderful Counselor, soften my heart when I am feeling betrayed. Your truth shows me that when Alexander did a "great deal of harm" to Your apostle Paul (2 Timothy 4:14–16), many deserted him. Perhaps the damage Alexander brought to Paul caused his arrest and imprisonment. How devastating that must have been, God. Maybe his friends were so frightened that no one dared come to his defense. Only You, sovereign Lord, know what happened. You gave Your faithful one, Paul, what he needed to stand his ground and forgive his weak-hearted companions.

Learning how Paul survived not only the persecution of his enemies but also the betrayal of his friends gives me tools to better serve You. Your truth tells me,

The Lord stood at my side and gave me strength, so that through me the message might be fully proclaimed and all the Gentiles might hear it. And I was delivered from the lion's mouth (2 Timothy 4:17 NIV).

Your Word, O Prince of Peace, opens my eyes. It's not about my hurt feelings or the sting of betrayal; it's all about Your message of salvation that needs to be shouted into the world of darkness.

You, Jesus, the One who endured persecution from friend and foe, knew exactly how to strengthen Paul in his time of need. You were his example! Thank You for being the example he needed. Paul wanted Timothy to know—and You want me to know too—that even when friends and other people fail us, You are the rock, You are the faithful friend. You alone are the tower of refuge.

So as I meditate on Your powerful words and follow You, my Shepherd, I am able to rest. I can forgive others' failings because I know Your grace is sufficient.

· · · · · · · · · · · · · · · · · ·

Direct my footsteps according to your word;
let no sin rule over me.
PSALM 119:133 NIV

You Fulfill Your Promises

{ TITUS }

You never fail me! When I seek Your Word, the Bible, it's easy to trace Your promises from the Old Testament to their fulfillment in the New Testament. In hindsight, the signs of Your coming seem so blatant, I wonder how Your people of Israel missed them—and how they still couldn't see the end result when the You, the Messiah, finally did come.

I wonder why people can't see Your truth now. You are alive and everywhere! But, thousands of years have passed since Your birth. Life has continued, generations have come and gone, and it seems like everything will continue on as is, even though You have told us—told me—otherwise.

You have said from the very beginning that You will put an end to sin, death, and separation when You return the second time. You have promised that those who trust in You will have eternal life with You. Though the fulfillment of those promises is taking a long time in my estimation, You are still faithful. Paul assured Titus that God "does not lie." Your truth tells me,

> When the kindness and love of God our Savior appeared, he saved us, not because of righteous things

we had done, but because of his mercy. He saved us through the washing of rebirth and renewal by the Holy Spirit, whom he poured out on us generously through Jesus Christ our Savior, so that, having been justified by his grace, we might become heirs having the hope of eternal life. This is a trustworthy saying. And I want you to stress these things, so that those who have trusted in God may be careful to devote themselves to doing what is good. These things are excellent and profitable for everyone (Titus 3:4–8 NIV).

I have trusted!

Your love never ends. One day I will be ushered into eternal fellowship with You in heaven. What a magnificent day that will be.

. . . .

This is good and acceptable in the sight
of God our Savior, who desires all men to be saved
and come to the knowledge of truth.
1 TIMOTHY 2:3–4 NASB

You Welcome Him

{ PHILEMON }

You know it doesn't come easy. Forgiving those who have hurt me is sometimes next to impossible. The more I think about it, the more I focus on my pain. I want revenge. But then I read Your truth in the book of Philemon.

You have shown me, through this small letter written by Paul, what forgiveness looks like. When Onesimus, a slave belonging to Philemon, deserted and sinned against his master—an offense punishable by death—his life was in jeopardy. But during his escape, Onesimus met Paul. (I can just imagine meeting Paul and learning from him!)

After hearing Your truth of forgiveness, grace, and mercy through Your Son, Onesimus embraced Jesus as his Savior and repented of his sins. Lord, how easy it would have been to run. But instead, he returned home and faced the consequences of his disobedience. He had the support and encouragement of Paul. Oh, how I would love that kind of support.

Lord, You amaze me how You orchestrate Your will in the lives of Your children. Paul had already led Philemon to You! Had Paul not witnessed to him, Philemon would have never known You—the one true God—or Your saving grace and the freedom found only in Your Son, Jesus. Now, Paul challenged, it was time for Philemon to offer that same kind of freedom to Onesimus:

> So if you consider me a partner, welcome him as you would welcome me. If he has done you any wrong or owes you anything, charge it to me (Philemon 1:17–18 NIV).

Lord, I can identify with Philemon, Onesimus, and Paul! I see myself as all three! I, too, was a slave to sin, but by Your loving grace and mercy, I am now free! So now will I extend forgiveness to those who have hurt me? And will I be like Paul and share Your amazing truth with others? Help me to be like Paul. What a majestic example You have shown me through his letter to one person.

. . . .

Having purified your souls by your obedience to the truth
for a sincere brotherly love, love one another earnestly
from a pure heart, since you have been born again,
not of perishable seed but of imperishable,
through the living and abiding word of God.
1 Peter 1:22–23

You Protect My Eyes

It takes just one look. One look away from Your unfailing love to change the course of a life. Heavenly Father, I hear about it. I see it. It's everywhere—even in the lives of Your followers. Adultery is tearing families apart.

David, Your chosen king, Your anointed one, was no exception. One glance at Bathsheba, and he had to find out who she was. He simply had to have her. And the rest history—adultery, an innocent man's death, and the loss of David and Bathsheba's child. A life in chaos.

Heavenly Father, when I think about the story of adultery, I have to go back to where sin started—the garden of Eden. Adam and Eve took their eyes off Your love and protection and were enticed to choose something hyped up to be better than You. Oh, the deception!

From there Your children, the Israelites, time and time again committed adultery against You—choosing the love of idols and pagan worship over Your love. And I, too, know that if I do not seek You, Your wisdom and love, I could fall into the same deception that would bring chaos into my life.

You are our one true love. And Satan, who targets our souls, looks for our weaknesses and uses them to tempt us to destroy our spiritual walk with You. Out of his deception we develop adulterous hearts! But You, God, are forgiving and loving to those who repent and seek after Your heart. Your truth tells me,

> I will be merciful toward their iniquities, and I will remember their sins no more (Hebrews 8:12).

You know that Your children are not perfect—that we will fail if we take our eyes off of the One who paid the price for our sins, Jesus. I want to become one with You and righteous in Your sight. I will be faithful to my true love—You.

. . . .

Today, if you hear his voice, do not harden
your hearts as in the rebellion.
HEBREWS 3:15

You Expose My Heart

Lord, I will praise You in my raging storms. I will lift my hands to You as the wind and hail hit against the essence of my being. O heavenly Father, I stand firm even knowing that there is thunder and lightning in the distance and the enemy is after our souls—he's coming after mine. Seeking to destroy the people You love, he speaks lies into our lives, leading our feet off the path of Your truth. But You are the Almighty, and You reign on Your throne!

So much of the hurt and destruction I see around me is the fallout of believing the lies of the world, of Satan, instead of Your truth. And every time I take a step in the wrong direction, siding with the enemy instead of You, my heart grows harder and the deception grows stronger. O Lord, I seek Your face and Your perfect path for my life.

You remind me that the power of Your Word is mightier than the enemy's schemes. You say that You are alive and actively at work in believers' lives, in my life, helping me to discern truth from error. Your Word isn't a historical idea; it is a sharp sword, piercing directly into my heart, exposing sin for what it really is. Your truth tells me,

The word of God is alive and active. Sharper than any double-edged sword, it penetrates even to dividing soul and spirit, joints and marrow; it judges the thoughts and attitudes of the heart. Nothing in all creation is hidden from God's sight. Everything is uncovered and laid bare before the eyes of him to whom we must give account (Hebrews 4:12–13 NIV).

Painful though it may sometimes be, the exposure of my worldly thoughts and actions is exactly what I need so that I won't slip into deception. But if I do, I can come to You in true repentance—knowing as my hands are lifted up to You, I'll receive Your perfect restoration. My storm will calm. My faith is in You.

. . . .

Without faith it is impossible to please God, because anyone who comes to him must believe that he exists and that he rewards those who earnestly seek him.
HEBREWS 11:6 NIV

You Count It All Joy

{ JAMES }

Trials aren't fun. Father, to be honest, if I see one coming, I make every effort to avoid it. I question You, Lord, when I read Your words spoken through Your servant James that tell me to consider trials as "pure joy." Really? Pure joy?

You gently remind me of my past trials and how You were in the midst of them. You show me Your perspective: that difficulty and struggle are not necessarily the enemy, that sometimes You are molding my character. You are teaching me not to sin during my trials but to seek You so that I will possess everything I need in life. Your wisdom helps me to discern the challenges I face. Your truth tells me,

> Count it all joy, my brothers, when you meet trials of various kinds, for you know that the testing of your faith produces steadfastness. And let steadfastness have its full effect, that you may be perfect and complete, lacking in nothing (James 1:2–4).

Though life is sometimes difficult, I am learning total reliance upon You. So as my faith grows in Your love, so does my perseverance. I know that You are transforming me into

Your likeness—a complete follower who has been nourished by Your great faithfulness in the midst of my trials. There is no doubt that when I look back on my challenges, I will see Your hand of goodness and remember Your Word: "Do not be conformed to this world, but be transformed by the renewal of your mind, that by testing you may discern what is the will of God, what is good and acceptable and perfect" (Romans 12:2). Knowing Your truth, I can handle anything.

. . . .

If any of you lacks wisdom, let him ask God,
who gives generously to all without reproach,
and it will be given him.

JAMES 1:5

You Are Unseen

{ 1 PETER }

Your followers gather in homes and churches around the world to sing songs of praise—to listen and to know Your truth. They pray out loud and study Your Word. I do the same thing. You are constantly on my mind as I praise You every day. Oh, how I love You and love to study Your Word.

But there are those who are outside looking in at us—looking at me—and wondering why so much time and energy are spent on someone no one in this world can even see. It's understandable, if You think about it. Truth is, they don't get it because they don't seek You. They don't know You!

Those of us who belong to You seek Your truth, seek Your face. But You have chosen to hide your appearance for right now. Though I long to see Your face—and know that one day I will—I know for now You are glorified and pleased by my faith in You. And through my faith and my love for You, I can develop an intimate relationship with You, sight unseen. Now. Today. By spending time in Your Word, in which You reveal Your heart, Your wisdom. Your truth tells me,

Though you have not seen him, you love him; and even though you do not see him now, you believe in

165

him and are filled with an inexpressible and glorious joy, for you are receiving the end result of your faith, the salvation of your souls (1 Peter 1:8–9 NIV).

Lord, Your Spirit resides within me, opening my spiritual eyes to see Your hand working in my life in very visible ways. Your presence and almighty power surround me in the beautiful world that You created. I will forever set my sights on You and wait for opportunities to share Your truth and Your love with others. No more misunderstandings.

. . . .

You have said, "Seek my face." My heart says to you,
"Your face, LORD, do I seek."
PSALM 27:8

You Empower Me

{ 2 PETER }

I try not to be judgmental because I know how it feels to be judged. Lord, I always seek the best in everyone, but I'm puzzled. There are those who call themselves Christians, who praise You for all to hear, then go on with their lives and continue to blatantly sin. Then there are those who truly seek to follow Your precepts but continue to live defeated lives, bound as prisoners to their sin.

Remind me as many times as it takes that not all those who acknowledge You or even praise Your name know You. Some of them do not seek Your truth. And those who do know You, who love and follow You but are in bondage to sin, they neglect to grasp an important truth: Not only are they forgiven, they are empowered. They just forget.

Lord, You are speaking to me! I often fail to remember that I am empowered. Heavenly Father, Your Spirit lives in me, causing Your Word to renew and release every area of my life once held captive. I am equipped to tear down the walls that keep me from being all that You have intended. Your truth tells me,

His divine power has granted to us all things that pertain to life and godliness, through the knowledge of him who called us to his own glory and excellence (2 Peter 1:3).

My almighty God, it is the same power that raised Your Son, Jesus, from the dead that now dwells in me! How can I stay stuck in sin any longer?

I have Your guidance and Your power to say no to sin and yes to Christ. I am empowered! I can live life worthy of what You have called me to do. I can strip off the old nature and live fully for You in my new life—my new life with You!

. . . .

If the Spirit of him who raised Jesus from the dead dwells in you, he who raised Christ Jesus from the dead will also give life to your mortal bodies through his Spirit who dwells in you.

ROMANS 8:11

You Know My Heart

{ 1 JOHN }

Lord, I am so thankful and blessed that I know You, that I live in Your light. I reminiscence about that day long ago when I bowed my knees and surrendered my life to You. You were waiting for me with open arms. And in that moment, I knew my world was about to change. No more living in the darkness.

Jesus, many years have passed since that day. I can't say that I've been perfect. You know that I haven't because You are sovereign and my God who is all-knowing. When I read the apostle John's first letter, my eyes focus on one word that is repeated throughout his message: *know*.

Lord, I am in awe that You know me and waited so long for me to know Your truth. You call me Your child even when I stumble. You know my heart and my love for You. Your truth tells me,

> Whoever keeps his word, in him truly the love of God is perfected. By this we may know that we are in him: whoever says he abides in him ought to walk in the same way in which he walked (1 John 2:5–6).

Today, I pray for those who don't know You and those who are afraid to surrender their lives because of the world's deception. Lord, use my life that You embraced to proclaim Your holy name and Your truth:

> If we say we have no sin, we deceive ourselves, and the truth is not in us. If we confess our sins, he is faithful and just to forgive us our sins and to cleanse us from all unrighteousness. (1 John 1:8–9).

O Almighty God, I know that You are waiting for them too.

. . . .

Whoever says "I know him" but does not keep
his commandments is a liar, and the truth
is not in him, but whoever keeps his word,
in him truly the love of God is perfected.

1 John 2:4–5

You Are the Love of My Life

{ 1 JOHN }

As I close my eyes and feel the touch of the breeze on my face, I feel the warmth of Your love—a love like no other. Your tender arms embrace me, pulling me close to Your heart. I hear Your Spirit whisper that You will never leave me. You will never forsake me. Nothing can separate me from You and Your unconditional love. I cling to Your Word: "For I am convinced that neither death nor life, neither angels nor demons, neither the present nor the future, nor any powers, neither height nor depth, nor anything else in all creation, will be able to separate us from the love of God that is in Christ Jesus our Lord (Romans 8:38–39 NASB).

Lord, the world longs to be in love. Everywhere I look, I find people searching for the perfect person to fulfill them, but they end up with superficial and empty relationships. If only they could grasp who You are, God. It's impossible to experience true love without You. We love because You first loved us. You *are* love! It's that simple. But people don't understand. We are incapable of loving one another if we don't know You! Your truth tells me,

Dear friends, let us love one another, for love comes from God. Everyone who loves has been born of God and knows God. Whoever does not love does not know God, because God is love (1 John 4:7–8 NIV).

You tell me that if I acknowledge that Jesus is Your Son, You live in me and I live in You. And whoever lives in love lives in You, and You in them. I live in love! I live in You! Our hearts beat as one. Now I am able to love others with a love that is unbreakable. What more in life do I need? I want to shout it at the top of my lungs!

· · · · · · · · · · · · · · · · · · ·

Dear children, let us not love with words
or speech but with actions and in truth.
1 John 3:18 NIV

You Protect My Heart

{ 2 JOHN }

His letter was short, but his words hit hard. Living in a self-centered culture where power and status rule, John's second letter to one of the ladies in the church speaks volumes to my heart. Even today, deceivers and false teachers mislead and trick us. Lord, I am to love others, but how can I love those who lie? And how do I protect my heart from their deceptions?

Your Spirit whispers to my heart: discernment. You reveal that others may creatively devise philosophies or strategies of godliness, but they lack Your truth and power because they are based in lies. John urged the lady and her family to hold firmly to Your gospel and to live lives characterized by Your love. Your truth tells me,

> And now, dear lady, I am not writing you a new command but one we have had from the beginning. I ask that we love one another. And this is love: that we walk in obedience to his commands. As you have heard from the beginning, his command is that you walk in love (2 John 1:5–6 NIV).

I feel You urging me to do the same. In the end, the life that radiates Your light and Your love will silence the futile efforts made by others to avoid Your gracious plan: salvation by faith alone in Your Son. "And so we know and rely on the love God has for us. God is love. Whoever lives in love lives in God, and God in them" (1 John 4:16 NIV).

Father, You never fail! You are love. And You protect me as I walk in Your love and lead others from deception to truth, which is eternal life with You through Your Son, Jesus.

. . . .

To the lady chosen by God and to her children,
whom I love in the truth—and not I only, but also
all who know the truth—because of the truth,
which lives in us and will be with us forever.
2 JOHN 1:1–2 NIV

You Commend Our Actions

{ 3 JOHN }

Search my heart, O Lord, if I ever disrespect or criticize my friends who walk with You! I've seen it happen many times—even to those in ministry. Fellow believers start out loving one another and knowing Your truth, but then power and greed take over and they forget their calling. Or jealousy and competition destroy Your purpose for their lives.

Lord, You stir my heart through John's letter to Gaius. Courageously, he took a stand against Diotrephes when he saw that Your missionaries were not being treated with love. Lord, I long for the same courage.

I love the wisdom that You give Your followers, and I'm amused how You put Diotrephes in his place through John's words to Gaius. He commended him! If only all of Your children would encourage each other like Gaius and realize that all believers are united as one in Your family. I pray that I will always respect and love others—believers and those who don't know You. I would never want my actions to cause anyone to question my faith in You. Your truth tells me,

Therefore we ought to support people like these, that we may be fellow workers for the truth (3 John 8).

Lord, no matter where a person is in their own faith walk—whether a new believer, a lifetime Christian, a missionary, or someone who is just now seeking You—I am called to evangelism in love. I am to support and uplift others! Lord, I will encourage my Christian friends who continue in the truth and walk in the light and love that come from You, to whom they all belong.

. . . .

I have no greater joy than to hear that
my children are walking in the truth.
3 John 4

You Motivate Me

{ JUDE }

How am I to respond to those who question the hypocrisy in the church or the ministry? What do I say to allegations that another believer has fallen into deception? Church is supposed to be a spiritual safe zone—the place where believers can rest and uplift one another from a harsh world. Lord, protect us!

Jude felt the same way, and through his letter he lets me know that not even the church is perfect this side of heaven. He was dealing with imposters who had invaded the church. Perverting the gospel of Your Son, Jesus Christ, with their own twist on grace, these people were dividing and threatening the church.

While the true church should be a haven of peace for Your people, Jude reminds me that there will scoffers and deceivers in the church. Lord, it's sad. And it breaks my heart that I have to be on guard. But on the other hand, it motivates me to test everything I'm taught and compare it to Scripture—Your Word! And I love Your Word!

O my mighty Defender, even though this hypocrisy exists, I stand firm in my faith and remain in Your love. Your truth tells me,

It is these who cause divisions, worldly people, devoid of the Spirit. But you, beloved, building yourselves up in your most holy faith and praying in the Holy Spirit, keep yourselves in the love of God, waiting for the mercy of our Lord Jesus Christ that leads to eternal life (Jude 19–21).

I will walk in the way that You have designed for Your people so that no one will ever question my actions or words. They will know I am Yours: "For I will proclaim the name of the Lord; ascribe greatness to our God! The Rock, his work is perfect, for all his ways are justice. A God of faithfulness and without iniquity, just and upright is he" (Deuteronomy 32:3–4).

. . . .

Let the words of my mouth and the meditation
of my heart be acceptable in your sight,
O LORD, my rock and my redeemer.

PSALM 19:14

You Are the Alpha and Omega

{ REVELATION }

Revelation can be an intimidating book for those who don't seek You. And for those who are lost, the book is nothing but doom and gloom. But I see You. I see hope. It is in Jesus—my Savior.

From the beginning to the end of Your Word, I see You at work in the lives of Your people. Now in Revelation, through John's vision of the unseen realms of heaven, I get a bigger glance of You than ever before. Though You are beyond my intellectual grasp, You want me to have a glimpse of what is to come. You want me to see the glory and majesty that lie behind this earthly veil. Like a zipper pulled down, the fabric of this realm slightly exposed, You allow me a peek into a greater reality that exists right now, right where I am, even though I don't see it with my physical eyes.

I see You. And You are seated on Your throne, ruling with absolute authority and power. There is none other like You. You are so perfect that the angelic creatures worshiping around Your throne never stop saying, "Holy, holy, holy is the Lord God Almighty."

O holy God, through Your holiness You give me hope! Your truth tells me,

> The seventh angel sounded his trumpet, and there were loud voices in heaven, which said: "The kingdom of the world has become the kingdom of our Lord and of his Messiah, and he will reign for ever and ever" (Revelation 11:15 NIV).

One day the world as we know it will end. Sin will lose its grip. Satan, the great deceiver, will be exposed and condemned to eternal punishment. Pain, sadness, and death will all vanish. I will finally see You and live with You for eternity. My praises will never end because You are "the Alpha and the Omega, the Beginning and the End" (Revelation 21:6), forever worthy of praise.

· · · · · · · · · · · · · · · · · · ·

The revelation from Jesus Christ, which God gave him
to show his servants what must soon take place.
He made it known by sending his angel to his servant John.
Revelation 1:1 NIV

You Separated Me

{ CONCLUSION }

In the beginning, heavenly Father, You were there. Complete darkness, total silence. Emptiness. And then You opened Your mouth and declared: *"Let there be light!"* Your very first words spoken. Then You separated light from darkness. As I come to the end of Your Word, the Bible, I know that Your radiant light didn't come from the sun or the moon, it comes from Your Son, Jesus Christ—the Savior of the world. The One who radiates Your light in a world full of darkness. My Savior!

I think about the blind man that Jesus healed. He was born blind. He lived in darkness. He neither knew nor experienced anything different. But then he met Jesus. And his life was changed forever:

> "As long as I am in the world, I am the light of the world." Having said these things, he spit on the ground and made mud with the saliva. Then he anointed the man's eyes with the mud and said to him, "Go, wash in the pool of Siloam" (which means Sent). So he went and washed and came back seeing (John 9:5–7).

Lord, we live in a world that is covered with mud—a matter that if placed over eyes that were not already blinded would cause darkness. But You wanted me to see You, to know You and to seek Your truth. You sent Your precious Son—the Son of God—into my life that was once dark, and declared: *"Let there be light!"* I embraced Your light, and my life was changed forever.

O heavenly Father, as I come to the end of Your Book, this is the beginning of my new life. I realize that through Jesus, I am no longer separated from You. In the beginning, You separated the darkness from light. You separated me. I no longer live in darkness. I live in Your light. I live in Your truth. A truth that has no end.

. . . .

Forever, O LORD, your word is firmly fixed in the heavens.
PSALM 119:89

About the Author

TERRY SQUIRES is a veteran author and creator of various gift products for teens and adults. She is the author/creator of the bestselling *TodaysGirls.com* series of twelve mysteries and a coordinating journal for teen girls. She also authored the *Communicate Christ* series, *God's Stories—My First Thoughts*, *Bible Stories for Bedtime*, *Ancient Heroes*, and contributed to the *ONE Impact* Bible.

Currently, Terry hosts the *Today's Life—Stories of Unshakable Faith* television program and mentors thousands to seek God's truth on her online ministry and website, I Seek Truth. She is a BSN graduate of Valparaiso University and is Registered Nurse. Terry lives in Nashville, Tennessee, with her husband, Ted. Together, they have four grown sons, three grandsons, and a Boston terrier named Reagan.

IF YOU ENJOYED THIS BOOK, WILL YOU CONSIDER SHARING THE MESSAGE WITH OTHERS?

Mention the book in a blog post or through Facebook, Twitter, Pinterest, or upload a picture through Instagram.

Recommend this book to those in your small group, book club, workplace, and classes.

Head over to facebook.com/worthypub, "LIKE" the page, and post a comment as to what you enjoyed the most.

Tweet "I recommend reading #ISeekTruth by @terrysquires // @worthypub"

Pick up a copy for someone you know who would be challenged and encouraged by this message.

Write a book review online.

Visit us at worthypublishing.com

twitter.com/worthypub

worthypub.tumblr.com

facebook.com/worthypublishing

pinterest.com/worthypub

instagram.com/worthypub

youtube.com/worthypublishing